✳ *Influential Asians* ✳

YO-YO MA

Grammy Award-Winning Cellist

Jeanne Nagle and
Lisa A. Chippendale

 Enslow Publishing
101 W. 23rd Street
Suite 240
New York, NY 10011
USA
enslow.com

Published in 2017 by Enslow Publishing, LLC.
101 W. 23rd Street, Suite 240, New York, NY 10011

Library of Congress Cataloging-in-Publication Data

Names: Nagle, Jeanne, author.| Chippendale, Lisa A., author.
Title: Yo-Yo Ma : Grammy award-winning cellist / Jeanne Nagle and Lisa A. Chippendale.
Description: New York, NY : Enslow Publishing, 2017. | Series: Influential Asians |
Includes bibliographical references and index.
Identifiers: LCCN 2015050586 | ISBN 9780766078994 (library bound)
Subjects: LCSH: Ma, Yo-Yo 1955—Juvenile literature. | Cellists—Biography—Juvenile
literature.
Classification: LCC ML3930.M11 N34 2017 | DDC 787.4092—dc23
LC record available at http://lccn.loc.gov/2015050586

Printed in the United States of America

To Our Readers: We have done our best to make sure all websites in this book were active and appropriate when we went to press. However, the author and the publisher have no control over and assume no liability for the material available on those websites or on any websites they may link to. Any comments or suggestions can be sent by e-mail to customerservice@enslow.com.

Portions of this book appeared in the book *Yo-Yo Ma: A Cello Superstar Brings Music to the World.*

Contents

Foreword

They say that you cannot really know a person until you spend time with him or her. When I worked for the Rochester Philharmonic Orchestra in the early 1990s, I spent time with, and consequently got to know, many celebrities and musicians—including world-class cellist Yo-Yo Ma.

In addition to being incredibly talented, Ma turned out to be everything one might hope: kind, thoughtful, gracious. What I did not expect was how funny he could be, almost a little goofy. One example of his sense of humor occurred when we were driving to a performance. "Disguised" in a pair of wrap-around sunglasses, he decided to call himself Bubba. As this supposedly anonymous person, he waved to people on the street as we drove to Eastman Theatre, calling, "Hey, hi," to them out the open car window.

Once on stage, however, Ma was nowhere near anonymous. Hearing and watching him play in the packed theater was thrilling. Backstage, after performing, he appeared to be in a trance, no doubt swept away by the music himself.

Yo-Yo Ma is dedicated to music in all its forms. He also is understandably proud of his Chinese heritage, which influences his work and other aspects of his life. From his Silk Road Ensemble, noted for performing music with an Asian "flair," to being a founding member of the Committee of 100, a nonprofit that addresses concerns of Chinese-Americans, Ma has proven himself a capable and enthusiastic representative of Asian culture.

Of course, to me, he'll always be plain old Bubba.

Yo-Yo Ma plays a child's cello while store patrons look on at a New York City music store in 1998. Ma has devoted his life not only to mastering the cello, but also to bringing music to the public.

Chapter 1

SHARING THE "SUITE" LIFE

ew York City had seen its share of street performers, but perhaps none quite like this. In
1997, classical music icon Yo-Yo Ma had sta-
tioned himself in the middle of a busy intersection near
Manhattan's Times Square. His cello case was open,
empty except for a sign thanking passers-by for any
spare change they might drop onto its felt lining. The
cello itself was in his capable hands. Ma was performing
a piece by Johann Sebastian Bach—as a panhandler, or
beggar.

This scene was not a way to raise money for
struggling symphony orchestras, nor was it merely a
stunt. Ma was filming an episode named "Six Gestures"
for a PBS special series, which aired in April 1998. There
is a logical explanation as to why this classically trained

cellist was scrounging for change in Times Square as part of a film, rather than appearing on stage with a world-class orchestra. Ma has long been interested in taking risks and exploring different kinds of music and ways of performing. "Six Gestures" was an experimental way of sharing his art and passion with others.

Meaningful Music

The six suites written by Bach for solo cello are very important to Yo-Yo Ma. Each suite is made up of six different sections, called movements, and is about twenty to thirty minutes long. The suites were among the first pieces of music that Ma learned when he started playing the cello at age four. He recorded all six suites soon after he became a professional cellist, and the recording won him his first Grammy Award. One of the movements from the Fifth Cello Suite was the last piece of music Ma played for his father before he died. It is no wonder, then, that he chose this music, by this composer, to be the subject of the experimental piece of performance art that became the *Inspired by Bach* series on PBS.

Mixed Media

In the early 1990s, Ma decided he wanted to see how creative artists who were not musicians would interpret the cello suites.[1] He approached film directors, dancers, and a garden designer, among others, about making a series of films based on the six cello suites by Bach. In the first installment of the six-part venture, "Six Gestures," Ma chose to work with British ice dancers Jayne Torvill and Christopher Dean. The pair dominated world ice-dancing competition in the early 1980s. Torvill and Dean invented new routines for each movement of the Sixth Suite.

Ma made the films for television so that he could bring Bach to a new audience, one that avoids concert halls featuring traditional classical music.[2] But he also created the *Inspired by Bach* project to help him find new inspiration for the cello suites while collaborating with artists from nonmusical fields. "I actually believe that all the arts and sciences can be joined together under philosophy," he told the media prior to the premier of "Six Gestures," the first installment in the series.[3] At a later date, he added, "It made me an infinitely richer person, and I think a better musician."[4]

Ma, the Music-Video Star

"Six Gestures" is like a documentary and a music video rolled into one.

Ma is on camera throughout the film, sometimes speaking about Bach, but mostly playing his cello. The camera often shows his long fingers rushing up and down the fingerboard (neck) of the cello, or his bow moving deftly across and between the strings. Although he starts out in Times Square, he does not stay there for the entire film. Sometimes he is shown in black and white playing in a church, and other times he plays in full color on the gravel-coated roof of a city building with skyscrapers as his backdrop.

Although he was trained to play classical music, Ma has embraced many different forms from all over the world.

No Boundaries

Although Yo-Yo Ma was trained from an early age to be a classical cello player, he has refused to be hemmed in on the music front. In fact, the *Inspired by Bach* film series was just one of his many adventures outside the boundaries of the traditional concert hall. Although he became known for playing classical music, his musical style choices have varied greatly. Over the years he has embraced, and in many cases mastered, bluegrass, jazz, and Asian-inspired compositions as well as classical.

Much like his music, even Ma's heritage seems to defy, or challenge, classification. In interviews, much has been made of his "tricultural" background: He is Chinese, French by birth, and an American citizen. While he has frequently honored his Chinese roots, through civic participation in pro-Asia and Asian-American organizations as well as his music, he also has made a point of honoring all the elements that make him who he is. At his core, Ma is truly a citizen of the world.

Chapter 2

THE BIGGER, THE BETTER

Yo-Yo Ma comes by his talent for, and love of, music naturally. His father was the Chinese composer and violinist Hiao-Tsiun Ma. His mother, Ya-Wen Lo, was a singer from Hong Kong. Hiao-Tsiun and Ya-Wen met in the early 1940s at Nanjing University, where Ya-Wen was studying music and voice. Hiao-Tsiun was Ya-Wen's music theory teacher. The two married on July 17, 1949, in Paris, where they began their life together as husband and wife. Ya-Wen began using the name Marina Ma.

The couple's first child, a daughter, was born a little more than two years later, on July 28, 1951. Yeou-Cheng Ma soon showed a remarkable talent for music. She began playing piano and violin before she was three, and she made exceptional progress.

On October 7, 1955, in Paris, a fourth member was added to the Ma family. Marina and Hiao-Tsiun named their newborn son Yo-Yo. The syllable *Yo* means "friendship." "With me," Yo-Yo later joked, "they seem to have got lazy and been unable to think of anything else, so they added another Yo."[1]

Finding the Right Instrument

Yo-Yo soon proved every bit as talented as his older sister. He could sing in tune from a very early age because he had perfect pitch. This is a state in which a person does not sing any higher or lower than the written notes of music. He also could tell when other musicians were off-pitch, even if the tune they were playing or singing was unfamiliar to him.

The Mas soon started their young son on piano and violin, as they had his sister. He did well on both instruments, but he did not seem to have much enthusiasm for the violin. His parents were puzzled until three-year-old Yo-Yo announced, "I don't like the sound violins make; I want a big instrument!"[2]

Yo-Yo had just the instrument in mind. The story goes that, when he was four years old, he passed a huge double bass while walking through the Paris Conservatory, which is a type of arts school. The double bass is the largest string instrument that can be played with a bow, like a violin is. Young Yo-Yo wanted to play an instrument that was at least two feet taller than he was.

Yo-Yo kept nagging his parents for his "big instrument." Finally, they reached a compromise and agreed to get their son the next largest instrument, a cello.[3] The full name of the instrument is violoncello, but it is commonly shortened to just *cello*. The instrument was child-sized, meaning it was small enough for the four-year-old to handle. Yo-Yo later recalled that when he wanted to try playing the cello, the store at which they bought the instrument could not find a chair small enough for such a young musician. He wound up sitting on three telephone books stacked up on the floor.[4]

The "Break Down" Method

Now that Yo-Yo had chosen his instrument, his father wasted no time in beginning his son's lessons. He taught Yo-Yo and Yeou-Cheng himself, and also tutored his children in French and in Chinese history and writing. They spoke Chinese at home and learned about their Chinese heritage and culture. To teach them music, Hiao-Tsiun worked out a special method for teaching very young children. Yo-Yo had to memorize two measures of music a day. Each measure was only a few notes.

"My father used to say that nothing is really hard," Yeou-Cheng Ma told a reporter in 2014. "If anything is hard just cut it into four pieces, and if that's hard, cut it into sixteen pieces. Eventually you can conquer it."[5]

Yo-Yo later said, "I found this [teaching] method ideal because I didn't like to work hard. . . . When a problem is complex, you become tense, but when you break it down

Yo-Yo and Yeou-Cheng were introduced to music at a young age. Here, the children play for the Denver Symphony Orchestra in 1961.

into basic components you can approach each element without stress."[6] Yo-Yo would later use this "breaking it down into basic components" method during his solo career when he had to learn music in a short period of time.

Yo-Yo did not have to practice for very long—just ten minutes at a time was often enough. But he was expected to concentrate completely during that time. As Yo-Yo's ability grew, his father began teaching him one of Bach's solo cello suites using the two-measures-a-day method. He did this despite the fact that parts of the suites are hard to play even for professional cellists.

Although Yo-Yo worked hard at the cello, he was also very playful. He enjoyed singing songs, particularly one about frogs. He liked to jump around the room like a frog while he sang. And, like most younger brothers, Yo-Yo enjoyed tormenting his older sister. While she practiced piano, Yo-Yo would stand at the doorway and throw spitballs at her. Or he would crawl around at his sister's feet while she played. He liked to hold down the piano pedals so that Yeou-Cheng could not use them.

Now Appearing Onstage

Hiao-Tsiun's main instrument was violin, not cello, and soon he decided it was time for his son to study with a professional cello teacher. He chose Mme. Michelle Lepinte, a well-respected instructor, to teach four-year-old Yo-Yo to further master his instrument.

When Yo-Yo was five, he gave his first recital, at the Institute of Art and Archaeology at the University of

Musical Morse Code

Yo-Yo and Yeou-Cheng used to tease and bother each other, like any brother and sister. Yet they also looked out for each other. As their first music teacher, their father could put pressure on them from time to time. Yo-Yo and his sister made up a musical code that would help break the tension. If either played a certain combination of notes during a lesson, the other would come in the room and interrupt. This distracted their father, and gave the child being taught a much-needed break.[7]

Paris. He played one of the Bach suites he had so carefully learned, as well as other selections. He also played the piano. The audience applauded enthusiastically, and the concert was a great success.

Even though their son was very talented, Yo-Yo's parents decided not to overwhelm him with too many concert appearances. They limited his performances and continued his musical education.[8]

Still, Yo-Yo would soon find himself playing in another country. Before he was six years old, he and his sister gave several recitals in the United States. The first was in Rochester, New York, at Nazareth College. The Mas traveled there to visit Yo-Yo's uncle. Other recitals took place in New York City, where the Mas stayed for several days before their return flight to Paris. These concerts, too, were a success.

Coming to the United States

Soon after the family's trip to the United States, Hiao-Tsiun was offered a position as director of music and children's orchestra conductor at the Trent School, a private elementary school in New York City. He accepted, even though the family had not planned to move to the United States. He had long wanted to conduct a children's orchestra.[9]

After returning to France for the summer, the Mas moved to New York City in the fall of 1962. Yo-Yo's parents wasted no time in finding a top-notch cello teacher for their son. He began studying with well-known cellist Janos Scholz, who subsequently taught Yo-Yo for two years. He was impressed with the young boy's enthusiasm and talent. "He proved to be the most extraordinary, the most charming . . . little boy imaginable," he said. "He was so eager to acquire musical knowledge that he just lapped it up. . . . He was the ideal student, the student that a teacher always hopes for."[10]

It did not take long for the rest of the United States to discover just how talented the Mas were. Yo-Yo gave a private performance for the famous cellist Pablo Casals in his home. Casals then contacted Leonard Bernstein, conductor of the New York Philharmonic. Bernstein was also a composer and an internationally known figure in the music world. The musical *West Side Story* is his most famous work.

Bernstein included Yo-Yo and Yeou-Cheng, who would accompany Yo-Yo on the piano, in a benefit concert

Influential Spanish cellist Pablo Casals (1876–1973) heard the Ma children play and connected them with Leonard Bernstein.

in Washington, DC, on November 29, 1962. Titled *American Pageant of the Arts,* the nationally televised concert was a benefit for the National Culture Center. President John F. Kennedy and his wife, Jacqueline, were in attendance. When introducing the young musicians, Bernstein noted that the Ma family was Chinese, and had been living in France before coming to the United States with the hope of becoming US citizens. He noted that this made Yo-Yo "a highly international type."[11]

"Now here's a cultural image for you to ponder as you listen," he told the audience, "a seven-year-old Chinese cellist playing old French music for his new American compatriots."[12]

Leonard Bernstein was not the only famous musician who helped jump-start Yo-Yo's career. Violinist Isaac Stern had seen Yo-Yo perform in Paris. Stern called Yo-Yo "one of the most extraordinary talents of this generation."[13] He kept track of the budding prodigy in New York. When Yo-Yo was nine, Stern arranged for him to study with Leonard Rose, a well-known cello player who also taught at the Juilliard School. Juilliard is one of the most prestigious music schools in the world. Yo-Yo entered the school's Pre-College Division, which holds classes on Saturdays.

Special Appearances

In 1964, Yo-Yo's cello career hit several milestones. In February, he performed a cello concerto with the Doctors' Symphonic Orchestra—an amateur orchestra made up of doctors—in New York City. In a concerto, the cellist

Leonard Bernstein, shown here in 1960 with some young musicians, brought Yo-Yo and Yeou-Cheng to play for President John F. Kennedy and his wife.

sits by himself in front of the orchestra. His part, called the solo part, is the highlight of the piece of music and is often very difficult. This was Yo-Yo's first appearance as a cello soloist with an orchestra. He performed the Concerto No. 1 by French composer Camille Saint-Saëns (1835–1921). This piece is among the first concertos that cello students learn, because the part is not too hard.

Later that year, the Ma children appeared on NBC-TV's *The Tonight Show Starring Johnny Carson.*

In December 1964, Yo-Yo and Yeou-Cheng played in Carnegie Hall in New York City. They played a cello and piano duet called a sonata. They were among many performers in the concert, which was a benefit to help raise money for the school they were attending at that time, the École Française. Their performance was reviewed in the *New York Times.* Robert Sherman, the reviewer, was impressed by their performance. He wrote, "This is no children's piece, nor did they play it like children."[14]

Just Your Average Prodigy

Meanwhile, Yo-Yo and Yeou-Cheng attended school, just like other children their age. By the fifth grade, Yo-Yo was showing a rebellious streak. He began cutting classes. "I spent a lot of time wandering through the streets, mainly because I just wanted to be alone," he later explained.[15] Yo-Yo was confused. His Asian upbringing told him he should be obedient to his parents, quiet, and disciplined. His new American culture told him he should think for himself. "At home, I was to submerge my identity," Yo-Yo said. "You can't talk back to your parents—period. At school, I was expected to answer back, to reveal my individuality."[16]

In 1968, Yo-Yo switched to a different school, the Professional Children's School. He continued to skip classes, and eventually his teachers decided he must be bored. He was placed in an accelerated program so that he could graduate early.

At home, Yo-Yo's time was strictly managed. He practiced cello for a half hour before breakfast in the morning, then went to school. After school and a snack, Yo-Yo practiced cello for an hour, then did homework for at least two hours.

After dinner, Yo-Yo was allowed to watch television for a little while. His favorite programs were *Little House on the Prairie* and *Daniel Boone.* Then he spent more time on either homework or cello before going to bed. Later, Marina Ma said, "We didn't allow our children to have too many friends or to participate in too many outside activities. My Yo-Yo and Yeou-Cheng had no time for that."[17]

The Ma family's discipline was working wonders on Yo-Yo's cello playing. His skill was growing at a remarkable pace. His teacher, Leonard Rose, was astounded not only by Yo-Yo's talent, but by how well the boy always prepared for his lessons.[18] "By the time Yo-Yo was eleven or twelve," Rose later said, "I had already taken him through the most difficult études [musical exercises]. He may have one of the greatest techniques of all time. I'm always floored by it."[19]

Way Out West

When Yo-Yo was thirteen years old, he gave his first concert on the West Coast. In 1968, the family flew out to visit Marina's sister in Berkeley, California. While they were there, Yo-Yo played the Saint-Saëns concerto with the San Francisco Little Symphony. Critic Arthur Bloomfield of the *San Francisco Examiner* described his playing as "flawless" and "staggering." After this triumph, requests for concerts flooded into the Ma household. The San Francisco Symphony, a top orchestra, invited Yo-Yo to return to California in two years to play the Saint-Saëns concerto with them.

Yo-Yo's parents continued to limit his appearances. They did not want to exhaust Yo-Yo, and they believed his education—both scholastic and musical—was of utmost importance. They also knew it was best not to let audiences have their fill of Yo-Yo's talent. It was better to whet people's appetite and leave them eager for more.[20]

Chapter 3

LESSONS LEARNED

As Yo-Yo neared the end of his high school studies, his concert schedule grew busier. In March 1971, he performed a solo piece with the Harvard-Radcliffe Orchestra in Cambridge, Massachusetts. A month later, Yo-Yo returned to Cambridge to give a recital at Radcliffe College, the women's college affiliated with Harvard University. While there, he visited Yeou-Cheng, who was studying biochemistry and music at Radcliffe. During the visit, Yo-Yo decided he liked Harvard.[1]

On May 6, 1971, Yo-Yo gave his first professional recital at New York's famous Carnegie Recital Hall. The recital was a benefit performance for the Children's Orchestra, which his father directed. In June of that year, Yo-Yo graduated with his high school diploma from the

At the age of fifteen, Yo-Yo Ma graduated from New York's Professional Children's School, which allows flexibility to children who work as professionals in the arts.

Professional Children's School. He was only fifteen years old, and he felt he was not ready for a concert career.[2]

"Wild" Child

Luckily, Yo-Yo did not have to decide about his future right away. He spent the summer after high school graduation at a music camp called Meadowmount, in the Adirondack Mountains in Westport, New York. There, students spend seven weeks practicing, taking lessons, and playing chamber music. Chamber music is written for small groups of instruments in which each musician plays a different part.

Future Collaborator

A twenty-one-year-old pianist named Emanuel Ax heard the recital. "I remember saying, 'Someday I have to work with that person!'" Ax recalled years later.[3] This was approximately three years before Ax himself would become famous as a musician. In 1973, Yo-Yo began playing with Ax, whom he met at the Marlboro Music Festival, a summer program in Marlboro, Vermont, for talented music students and young professionals. They became close friends and, in 1975, formed the Ax-Ma duo. At Marlboro around that time, Yo-Yo also met violinist Young Uck Kim. The three men later formed a trio.

This was the first time Yo-Yo had ever been away from home on his own. In his own words, he "went wild."[4] He skipped rehearsals, drank beer, and even left his cello outside in the rain. Yo-Yo felt confused about his identity. He was trying to figure out what he believed in and cared about.[5] After Meadowmount, Yo-Yo knew he was still not ready to be a professional musician. He also did not want to attend a conservatory, or music school, like Juilliard, full-time. In the fall, he enrolled at Columbia University in New York City. He continued to take lessons with Leonard Rose in addition to classes at Juilliard. He soon dropped out of Columbia—without telling his parents.

Yo-Yo was also experimenting with alcohol. He obtained a fake ID card so he could buy alcoholic beverages, and he began drinking frequently with older friends. One day Ma got so drunk that he passed out in a practice room at Juilliard. He was rushed to the hospital, where doctors pumped his stomach. Because of this, he missed a rehearsal of the Children's Orchestra that his father conducted. His parents were deeply ashamed of his behavior. Fearing that he had set a bad example for Yo-Yo, his father gave up his daily glass of wine before dinner. Yo Yo felt embarrassed and guilty.[6] He stopped drinking after this incident.

Getting Inspired

During this difficult year, Yo-Yo was trying to decide whether he really wanted to become a musician. His experiences at Vermont's Marlboro Music Festival during the summer of 1972 helped him decide. There he spent hours playing chamber music with other young, talented musicians, sometimes rehearsing into the wee hours of the morning. Yo-Yo loved chamber music. "I thought there could be nothing better than to play string quartets [music for two violins, viola, and cello] for the rest of my life," he later told a reporter for *Strings* magazine.[7]

Yo-Yo was also inspired by Pablo Casals, revered as the world's greatest cellist in the first half of the twentieth century. "I didn't know I was definitely going to be a cellist; it was summers spent at Marlboro and other summer schools that were a tremendous inspiration to me," Yo-Yo later said. "To see someone like Casals stand up in front of the orchestra and scream at the top of his voice was catalytic [inspiring]. I thought that if [he] can feel that strongly about music at ninety-four then I can stick with this for the next 50 years."[8]

His first summer at Marlboro, Ma formed a close friendship with Jill Hornor, a violinist several years older than he was. She had just finished her sophomore year at Mount Holyoke, a women's college near Boston. Hornor was working in the office for the festival. "She was probably the first person who really wanted to find out what I truly thought," he said. "She used to say, 'What do you really mean by that?' That totally dumbfounded me."[9]

Following that summer at Marlboro, Yo-Yo finally decided what to do with the next few years of his life. He enrolled at Harvard, the ivy-league school located in Cambridge, Massachusetts, outside Boston. "Going there

Instruments in His Arsenal

As Ma was preparing to attend Harvard, his family obtained a fine cello for him in a shop in France. The cello was made in 1722 by an Italian instrument maker named Matteo Goffriller. Yo-Yo eventually nicknamed it "Sweetie Pie."

In 1984, he acquired a Davidoff Stradivarius cello, made in 1712. Stradivarius cellos and violins are considered to be the best in the world. He also owns a high-tech carbon-fiber cello made by Massachusetts instrument manufacturer Luis and Clark. This instrument is not as expensive as Yo-Yo's antiques, but it is able to withstand the bitter cold temperatures that could ruin a wooden cello.

was part of finding out whether I could do anything else but play the cello," he later said.[10]

On to Harvard

Word of Yo-Yo's playing spread quickly across the Cambridge campus. In his freshman year, one of his professors, Irven DeVore, a classical music fan, heard him play a concert at a nearby museum. The next day, Professor DeVore announced to the class that Yo-Yo's cello playing was better than that of the famous Pablo Casals. Yo-Yo was so embarrassed, DeVore told *Harvard Magazine*, that "the poor guy turned purple."[11]

During his first year at Harvard, Yo-Yo played some thirty concerts in venues all over the world. For the next three years of his undergraduate life, however, he found it easier to limit his out-of-town engagements to one a month. That restriction did not keep Yo-Yo from performing often at Harvard. He could be found playing cello nearly anywhere and everywhere, including dormitory common rooms and living rooms. All anyone had to do was ask and he would join the university's Bach Society orchestra for a performance, or accompany singers in campus productions of Gilbert and Sullivan shows.

His formal performances drew huge crowds. His senior roommate, Richard Kogan, remembers many people who could not get tickets to a concert jamming themselves into a small room in Memorial Hall to hear Yo-Yo play a pre-concert mini-show. The cellist played Bach concertos for half an hour, right up until the start

While pursuing his undergraduate degree, Ma played many concerts on the Harvard campus. He also continued to play engagements around the world.

time of the concert. *Harvard Magazine* quoted Kogan as saying, "Even then he felt it his mission to bring music to everybody."[12]

All of this playing—and the practicing he had to do—made it hard for Yo-Yo to spend a lot of time studying. He was able to juggle his music career with his academic studies because, he said, "I was unbelievably lazy in everything. I had very low standards—I didn't feel compelled to get high grades, or to practice many hours every day."[13] Each semester, he picked one class into which he would put a great deal of effort. Otherwise, Yo-Yo often waited until the last minute to complete assignments, writing papers late into the night. Once, he even picked the lock of the music library so he could stay up all night listening to the music assigned for that semester.

Occasionally, his bad study habits caught up with him. In his freshman year, Ma was placed on academic probation after sleeping through an exam. That meant that he could be forced to leave Harvard if his grades did not improve. Luckily, they did.

Courses of Study

Yo-Yo was curious about many different subjects when he went to Harvard. He majored in the humanities, which let him take classes in a wide variety of subjects, including history, German, sociology, fine arts, and literature. He was interested in different cultures because of his multicultural upbringing: His family was Chinese, he was born in France, and he was raised in America. He wanted to study what made other cultures different and what they had in common.[14] One of his favorite classes was an anthropology class taught by Professor DeVore. "My whole life was in a sense changed by that course," said Yo-Yo.[15]

Even though he was majoring in the humanities, Yo-Yo took many music classes at Harvard. There was only one class that taught music performance, a chamber music class taught by Leon Kirchner. Most of the music classes concentrated on analyzing the theory behind how music is written. At first, Yo-Yo did not want to learn too much about music theory. He was afraid that thinking too much about how music is constructed would hurt his instincts for cello playing.[16] He had several professors, such as composers Leon Kirchner and Luise Vosgerchian, who encouraged and pushed him to learn to analyze music. Eventually, Yo-Yo soon became fascinated by what he was studying.

Harvard Wrap-up

Even though Yo-Yo was very busy while he was at Harvard, he found time for one more commitment: his friendship with Jill Hornor. During Yo-Yo's freshman year, Jill went to Paris for a year of study abroad. The two began writing letters more and more frequently until each was writing a letter a day. Yo-Yo was accumulating hundreds of dollars in telephone bills with calls to France. At one point he even flew to Paris to spend a week with Jill. The next year, Jill returned to Mount Holyoke. After she graduated, she went to Cornell University, in Ithaca, New York, to do graduate studies in German literature. The two continued their long-distance relationship.

In 1976, Yo-Yo played for Mstislav Rostropovich, considered the greatest living cellist at the time, who was at Harvard to give a master class. In a master class, students play before other students and an audience, then receive advice and criticism from the teacher as the audience watches. Yo-Yo played the first movement of the cello concerto by Czech composer Antonín Dvoák for Rostropovich. It was the same piece Rostropovich himself was playing that week with the Boston Symphony. Rostropovich was very critical of Yo-Yo because he knew

Ma met Mstislav Rostropovich in a master class at Harvard. The Russian cellist agreed to take on Ma as a student.

Yo-Yo was very talented. He told him that his sound had no "center," meaning his playing was unfocused and lacked personality.[17] But by the end of the master class, the master cellist had offered to take Ma as a student.

In June 1976, Ma's Harvard years came to a close. He graduated with a bachelor of arts in humanities. Even though his grades were not the best, Yo-Yo felt that he had gotten what he needed out of his time at Harvard. "Ultimately," he said, "the purpose of college is to open your mind to different things, to disciplines you don't know anything about. That purpose was served."[18]

Chapter 4

THE START OF SOMETHING BIG

With his academic career behind him, it was time for Ma to begin his career as a performer. He hit the ground running, appearing with orchestras across the United States. He booked a few concerts in Europe also. Playing so much, in so many locations, was a lot like the way he approached music at Harvard. "I wanted to do everything, anything," Ma said of that exciting time in his professional life.[1]

His summers were spent playing chamber music and teaching at music festivals. Among the prestigious, or well-respected, festivals he attended were the Spoleto Festival U.S.A. in Charleston, South Carolina; the Aspen Music Festival in Aspen, Colorado; and the Tanglewood Music Festival in Lenox, Massachusetts. The location

No Place Like Home

Tanglewood long has been one of Ma's favorite places. His annual performances there date back to his son's infancy. "My son, Nicholas, was just three months old when I played at Tanglewood the first time," Ma said in June 2003, not long after Nicholas returned home from his second year at Harvard University.[2] The Mas purchased a summer home near Tanglewood so that Yo-Yo could spend as much time as possible with his family during the summer months.

"Maybe it's the hills but I get so calm and psyched when I get close to Tanglewood."[3]

of the last festival would become very near and dear to Ma's heart.

The Wedding March

Throughout his travels, Ma had kept in close touch with Jill Hornor. By the spring of 1977, the couple had been dating for nearly five years. At that point, a friend advised Ma that it was time he made the relationship official. "If you don't do something," he said, "fish swim away."[4]

Ma took his advice. He bought a ring and two plane tickets to Cleveland, where Jill's parents lived. Then he dressed in a suit and tie, took a bus from New York City to Ithaca, and rang Jill's doorbell. When she answered the door, Ma knelt and asked her to marry him. Jill said yes. The two then flew to Cleveland to share the happy news with her parents. On May 20, 1978, they were married.

Ma has found a sanctuary and a home away from home in Tanglewood, a renowned music venue located in the Berkshires in Massachusetts.

At first Ma's parents were not very happy about Yo-Yo's choice of bride. They had hoped their son would marry a Chinese woman. They worried that the couple's children would not learn Chinese traditions. Eventually they changed their minds and accepted Jill into the family.[5]

The newlyweds moved into Harvard's Leverett House, where they would live for the next three years. Jill was a German tutor, and Yo-Yo was one of the university's artists in residence. They had agreed to share the cooking and other household jobs, but this arrangement did not work as they had planned. First of all, as Ma himself admitted, "I've proved horrible at all domestic chores."[6]

Second, he spent very little time at home. His career was growing by leaps and bounds.

A Prized Artist

In April 1978, Ma gave a recital at New York's 92nd Street Y. The concert received a rave review from Joseph Horowitz, a critic for the *New York Times*. "Yo-Yo Ma . . . is a cellist of staggering ability," he wrote.[7] Ma was becoming quite well known.

Ma met Jill Hornor when they were both at the Marlboro Music Festival. They kept up their friendship long distance until it blossomed into romance and, eventually, marriage.

In addition to receiving excellent reviews for his concerts, Ma also won a prestigious award called the Avery Fisher Prize in 1978. The prize, awarded by New York's Lincoln Center, is given only to the most outstanding solo instrumentalists. Soon orchestras all over the world wanted Ma to perform with them. Every time Ma's agent called to offer him more concerts, he said yes. He did not think about how busy his schedule would become. For the first few years of his career, Ma played as many as 150 concerts a year. That averages out to nearly one concert every other day.

Each year, Ma chose two or three concertos to play during the concert season, choosing from among the twenty to thirty concertos he had already learned. Ma also tried to learn several new pieces each year, music written by contemporary composers. He even commissioned, or requested, new works from composers. He felt it was important to play new music—a sentiment he has carried for years. "Modern music is now much more accessible than it used to be," he told a reporter for *Stereo Review* magazine. "I hope people get excited when a composer writes a new piece."[8]

In addition to his solo appearances with various orchestras, Ma continued to play chamber music as often as he could. He began performing regularly with pianist Emanuel Ax in 1975. They played about ten concerts a year together. Sometimes they spent more time talking than playing during their rehearsals. "For the first couple of years, we had long discussions," said Ma. "We'd argue and argue, and realize after two and a half hours that we were actually using different words to describe the same thing."[9] Even though Ma was playing all over the world, he still found time to help out the college he had attended. In February 1980, he played with his old Harvard trio—violinist Lynn Chang and pianist Richard Kogan—to help raise money for a Harvard student service organization. He also played with the Harvard Chamber Orchestra, conducted by his former teacher Leon Kirchner.

Ma first teamed up with pianist Emanuel Ax at the Marlboro Music Festival, forming an essential relationship that would continue to the present day.

Career in Jeopardy

In April 1980, Ma's career was threatened by a medical condition. He had a severe curvature of the spine, called scoliosis, and time was running out to fix it. Doctors were worried the curve would become worse and eventually cause his spine to squeeze his internal organs. He needed to have an operation, and it was somewhat risky. There was a small chance that nerves could be damaged, preventing Ma from playing the cello again. Ma understood the risk. "I used to think that life ended with that operation," Ma said. "I didn't dare plan ahead. I was prepared to do something else afterwards, there was always this one percent chance something might go wrong."[10]

Luckily, the operation was a success. It even made Ma stand two inches taller. For six months after the surgery, his upper body was enclosed in a cast that went up to his neck. The doctors cut the cast in a shape that would allow Ma to practice the cello. He joked that he liked the cast. "With my cast on, I felt like a football player," he said. "I had broad shoulders, a fabulous physique."[11]

Ma gave a concert of the second Bach cello suite while he was still in the cast. Aside from that, Ma played very little during his recovery. "I didn't realize until after the operation that I had been in constant pain," he said a few years later. "Now, … I'll be able to play for many more years."[12]

A Little Help, Please

Even though Ma was considered one of the best, if not the best, cellists in the world, he still depended on former teacher Leonard Rose for occasional help. In January 1981, Ma paid him a visit. He was unhappy with his bow arm. After a few hours, Rose suggested Ma make a slight change to the way he held the bow. "Suddenly everything clicked!" he said.[13]

Full-Steam

After Ma's cast came off, he resumed his busy concert schedule. During the 1980–81 concert season, Ma played about 120 concerts all over the world. Most were solos with orchestras. He and Emanuel Ax began occasionally playing trios with violinist Young Uck Kim. A Beethoven recital Ma gave with Ax in Boston in 1981 was so popular that the location had to be changed from a small recital hall to Symphony Hall, the large concert hall where the Boston Symphony plays.

Because Ma did so much traveling, he sometimes had to cope with unexpected situations. Once, when he was traveling on Germany's notoriously fast-paced Autobahn highway, his car's tire went flat. While he waited for help, he decided to make use of the time. Seated on a suitcase by the side of the road, with cars whizzing by, he began practicing for a concert in Frankfurt that night. "People couldn't believe what they were seeing," said Ma.[14] Also in 1981, Ma took on a new challenge. He rewrote several violin pieces by the early-nineteenth-century composer and violinist Niccolò Paganini so that he could play them on the cello. These pieces were from Paganini's set of 24 Caprices, which are among the hardest pieces of music ever written for the violin. They would not become any easier when played on the cello.

"I made myself do them for some perverse reason," said Ma. "A week before I was to play them, I panicked. I started practicing four hours a day and developed a new muscle on my hand. When I got to the concert I almost had to be pushed out on stage. But I did it—for which I'm now grateful. Everything else is easy compared to that."[15]

That fall, the Mas moved out of Leverett House into a home in Winchester, Massachusetts. Jill had to start packing without her husband, although he did take a week off from practicing to help finish the move. They did not spend much time there at first. During the 1981–82 concert season, Jill took time off from teaching so she could join Yo-Yo on tour.

New Experiences

In 1983, Ma began a career as a recording artist. Among his first recordings were two of Beethoven's sonatas for cello and piano with Emanuel Ax, the Saint-Saëns and Lalo cello concertos with the National Orchestra of France, and the five Paganini caprices he had adapted. He was accompanied in the Paganini by pianist Patricia Zander, a longtime friend and collaborator. Ma also

Surgery to correct the scoliosis from which he suffered threatened to end Ma's career. However, he emerged stronger than before and resumed his busy concert and recording schedules.

recorded his favorite music, the Bach cello suites, for the first time.

Ma was enjoying something new and exciting in his family life, too. He became a father when he and Jill had their first child, Nicholas. After Nicholas's birth, Ma made a list of priorities in his life. Among the items on that list were guidelines for his musical career. "First of all, I promised myself that if I ever felt really burned out and lost enthusiasm for giving concerts I'd be responsible enough to quit," he told author David Blum. "Second, I decided that every concert I played—no matter where, no matter if the city was big or small—was going to be special."[16]

Ma began saying no to some concerts. He wanted to spend less time traveling. "Alone on tour you can get very self-centered," he said. "It's easy to think of nothing but music and planning. . . . It's important to get away from it. I'd like some vacation time, private time—to live some semblance of a good life."[17]

That would not happen in 1984, which was another very busy year. Ma stayed busy in the recording studio, including sessions to record two more Beethoven cello sonatas with Ax. He also experimented with jazz, making a recording of a suite for cello and jazz piano trio by contemporary composer Claude Bolling. The hard work apparently paid off. He won his first Grammy Award, for Best Classical Performance: Instrumental (without orchestra) for his recording of the Bach cello suites.

Not everything that happened to Ma in 1984 was good. That year he faced the loss of one of the most important musicians in his life. Former teacher Leonard Rose died after an illness of several months. "Leonard Rose was much more than my teacher," said Ma. "He was my mentor and my friend."[18] Now Ma would have to look elsewhere for musical companionship and advice.

Chapter 5

PUSHING MUSICAL BOUNDARIES

Sometimes a person can experience too much of a good thing. That is the situation Ma found himself in during the later portion of the 1980s. In particular, he was finding it hard to juggle his stellar career with his family life. Now the father of two—daughter Emily was born in 1985—Ma realized that something had to give. He made the decision not to book, or schedule, concerts that would take him away from home on his children's birthdays. Additionally, he set aside the entire month of July for vacation time with Jill and the kids.[1]

Although these scheduling tricks gave him much-needed time to decompress with family, in truth, they barely made a dent in Ma's demanding performance calendar. Ma was in great demand, as a soloist, chamber musician, and recording artist. He continued to play concertos with the world's best orchestras. In 1985 he went on tour with violist Kim Kashkashian and violinists Gidon Kremer and Daniel Phillips. The quartet's specialty was playing the last pieces that composers had written before they died. "If we had to find a name for ourselves," said Ma, "it would have been 'The Quartet That Plays Only the Late Works.'"[2] And, of course, Ma continued to take to the stage with his good friend and collaborator, Emanuel Ax.

On the recording front, Ma released his interpretation of Edward Elgar and William Walton concertos, which won a Grammy Award in 1985. Ma won two more

Ma didn't let the increasing demands on his career interfere with a strong family life. Here he stands with his wife Jill, daughter Emily, and son Nicholas in 2012.

Grammys for recordings completed with Ax, in 1985 and 1986. In 1987, the duo released a set of the complete Beethoven cello sonatas. Also, as part of the "Late Works" quartet, Ma recorded Shostakovitch and Schubert pieces, in 1989 and 1990, respectively.

Getting Jazzy

By the late 1980s, Ma was ready to try playing a completely different kind of music: jazz. After meeting jazz violinist Stephane Grappelli, Ma decided he wanted to work with him. The two men performed concerts together and recorded an album called *Anything Goes*. It featured arrangements of songs by famous jazz composer Cole Porter. Unlike most of Ma's other recordings, *Anything Goes* did not get very good reviews. Writer Ed Siegel of *The Boston Globe* later said, "His one attempt at jazz, 'Anything Goes' with Stephane Grappelli, was not a success because anything didn't."[3]

Jazz is different from classical music in many ways. One of the most important differences is that jazz performers make up, or improvise, some of the music during the performance. Jazz composers often write down only the main tune, then leave the rest up to the musicians. Classical musicians, on the other hand, play exactly what the composer wrote. The composer spells out every note from beginning to end. Ma was never trained to play jazz, but he did do a little bit of improvisation in his concerts with Grappelli. Ma did not try playing jazz very often after this. He enjoys listening to jazz, though. Among his favorite performers are

Ma's partnership with the late French jazz violinist Stephane Grappelli was not entirely successful.

Miles Davis, John Coltrane, and the Turtle Island String Quartet.

Preserving Cultural Roots

Despite a jam-packed schedule, Ma managed to make time for a cause that was near and dear to his heart. Together with Chinese-American architect I.M. Pei, he founded an organization known as the Committee of 100 in 1990. This group is made up of Americans of Chinese heritage who are leaders in various fields. Members seek to call attention to issues that matter to Chinese-Americans, including US relations with China and equal economic, employment, and educational opportunities for Asian-Americans.[4]

Specific program groups within the Committee of 100 oversee matters concerning trust-building between the United States and China; leadership and mentoring programs for Chinese-American students; and bringing about a greater feeling of inclusion for Chinese-Americans in US society. The organization is a nonprofit, and does not have ties to any political parties.

Forging Partnerships

Meanwhile, Ma continued his partnership with Emanuel Ax. In 1990 the two went on tour. After their performance at Avery Fisher Hall in May, critic Bernard Holland of the *New York Times* commented on how the friendship between the two men seemed to improve their music-making: "The two have played together for many years and it shows," Holland wrote. "[Their musical] phrases

... have an unusual sense of mutual understanding. One looks for a less corny way to explain this musical relationship, but friendship seems the only apt one."[5]

There may have been another reason for their excellent concerts besides just friendship, according to Ma. He said that after working together for so long, he and Ax had developed a kind of chamber music mental telepathy. "We ... have a built-in understanding," he said. "We can look at each other during a performance and know exactly what the other person is thinking."[6]

Ax and Ma often added other players to their duo to make trios and quartets, including violinists Young Uck Kim and Isaac Stern and violinist/violist Jaime Laredo. In 1991, a recording of two Brahms piano quartets played by Ma, Ax, Stern, and Laredo won a Grammy for Best Chamber Music Performance.

In the early 1990s, Ma formed another partnership with a completely different kind of musician. Singer and conductor Bobby McFerrin invited Ma to participate in a concert McFerrin was directing in San Francisco. McFerrin is best known for his 1988 album *Simple Pleasures*, which featured the hit song "Don't Worry, Be Happy."

McFerrin was conducting Beethoven's Seventh Symphony to celebrate his fortieth birthday. He had met Ma a few years earlier at Tanglewood, at a concert celebrating Leonard Bernstein's seventieth birthday. McFerrin wanted to improvise, or make up something on the spot, with Ma during the concert. When Ma explained that he did not improvise, McFerrin agreed to write something for voice and cello. He put it off until the day before the concert. Then, Ma said, "The day of the concert he changed everything."[7] The two ended up improvising together for twenty minutes. Ma said, "I'd never done this before and was shaking."[8]

"Coach" Ma

Among all of these concerts and recording projects, Ma still found time to educate young people about music. To reach young audiences, Ma appeared in children's music shows produced at Tanglewood. These were shown on the BBC television channels in England and on the Arts

As Ma's star rose, he broadened his exposure and diversified his collaborations. He even played the cello with the Muppet character Elmo on an episode of the children's educational show *Sesame Street*.

& Entertainment cable channel in the United States. He also appeared on children's programs like *Sesame Street* and *Mr. Rogers' Neighborhood*, where he played part of a Bach cello suite.

Ma wanted to help young cellists improve their playing, even though he did not have time to teach cello students on a regular basis.[9] Whenever his schedule would allow it, Ma stopped at universities and conservatories to give master classes. He would spend about half an hour with each student, letting each play his or her entire piece without interruption. Then he praised the positive aspects of the performance before offering suggestions to improve weaknesses. He encouraged students to relax and play as expressively as possible. Once, a boy struggling to play on a poor instrument, was given the chance to play his piece on Ma's own cello.[10]

Ma has been interested in teaching all young musicians, not just those who play the cello. Much of his teaching and coaching has taken place in the summer at the Tanglewood Music Festival. He often has coached student chamber music groups, and occasionally soloed with Tanglewood's youth orchestra. Music journalist Edith Eisler commented on one performance: "He treated them with total respect, inspiring them to give their best . . . and they obviously adored him."[11]

Marathon Man

The six Bach cello suites Ma had learned as a youngster remained an important part of his musical and personal life. In January 1991, he offered the suites to New York

Make Musicians, Not Competitors

Ma is often troubled by the training hopeful young musicians receive in conservatories. Most troubling seems to be the fact that top students are pushed to enter competitions. Ma hates competitions. He thinks the point system used to decide how well someone plays is too difficult and arbitrary, meaning done without necessarily being fair. Also, he thinks that the young musicians who win competitions have more important things to do in life rather than just playing concerts. "If you put a lot into producing concerts instead of trying to open yourself to learning different ways of making music, you'll be a diminished person."[12]

audiences in a new format—all in a row. In a marathon solo concert, Ma played all six Bach cello suites in one evening. Before he played, and during each intermission, he stretched and did deep breathing exercises to stay relaxed. He also ate very little. At 5 p.m., Ma began playing the first suite for a sellout crowd at Carnegie Hall in New York City. Four and a half hours after he began—including an hour-long dinner break and two intermissions—Ma played the last note of the sixth suite. The audience gave him a standing ovation.

After the concert, Ma went out with some friends to celebrate the performance. He returned at 3:00 in the morning to his wife's parents' apartment. They were asleep. The door was locked, and Ma realized that he had forgotten his keys. He did not want to wake anyone up by banging on the door, so he stretched out on the floor in the hallway and tried to sleep. It was not easy; maintenance men and newspaper delivery men were banging around in the elevator and in the halls, and it was very cold. Ma's surprised in-laws found him outside their door at 6:30 in the morning, when they stepped out for the newspaper.

"That concert had meant so much to me," said Ma. "I had never tried something like that before and it was exhausting. And then three hours later, I'm a homeless person. That's the life of a musician."[13]

Hyper Drive

Later in 1991, Ma became involved in a project that took inspiration from one of Bach's cello suites and combined it with modern technology. He premiered a piece by composer and Massachusetts Institute of Technology (MIT) professor Tod Machover, written for hypercello. The hypercello was an attempt to unite technology and music. Ma played an electric cello that was outfitted with sensors and hooked up to four computers. There were also sensors on the bow and on Ma's right wrist. It had taken a team of five people from the MIT Media Lab more than a year to assemble the hypercello and create software for it that could work as Machover intended.

The beginning of Machover's piece, called "Begin Again Again," is based on the sarabande movement from Bach's Second Cello Suite. The music came out different each time Ma played it. The computers reacted to the notes he played, how fast and loud he played them, and even what part of the bow he played them with. In the first movement, Ma used the electric cello. As the music begins, the cellist has a lot of control over what the computers do. But as the music continues, it gets faster and faster, with the computer music becoming wilder and wilder.

In the second movement, Ma played with the computers on his own nonelectric cello. Then he listened to the sounds coming out of the computers and tried to play with them. This movement, which was a series of variations on a theme, was much slower. Each computer was attended by an engineer who manually triggered sounds that failed to go off automatically.

"Begin Again Again" was part of a recital at Tanglewood of works by American composers. Also on the program were Ma's arrangement for cello of Leonard Bernstein's Clarinet Sonata and a piano trio by Charles Ives. These two pieces would later appear on Ma's 1993 recording *Made in America*. Soon the Bach suites would become even more meaningful to Ma. His father, who had first taught him the suites, suffered a severe stroke. It left him unable to walk or sit up, and made speaking difficult. Before he died on August 28, 1991, Hiao-Tsiun Ma made one last request of his son: play Bach. Ma played the sarabande movement from the Fifth Suite for his father before he died.

Projects Galore

Ma had no shortage of other projects during that time. In 1992, Ma and Bobby McFerrin teamed up in the recording studio to make a duet album called *Hush*. Several of the pieces on the CD are interpretations of classical pieces that showcase McFerrin's remarkable vocal abilities. Other pieces are folk tunes arranged by McFerrin or his original compositions. The CD sold very well, spending thirty-three weeks at the top of *Billboard* magazine's classical crossover chart. Several years later, the album would be certified as a gold record, meaning it had sold 500,000 copies.

Grammy Award–winner Bobby McFerrin has collaborated with Ma on several occasions. The vocalist and conductor is known for his remarkable vocal range and unique style.

Ma also played "Begin Again Again" several more times. The European premiere of the work was in Amsterdam, the Netherlands, in 1993. It took Machover's team from MIT Media Lab four days to get the complex hypercello system working in the Amsterdam concert hall, called the Concertgebouw. It was not ready until the night before the concert.

Ma saw Machover's hypercello piece as an interesting experiment. "I have two hopes for it," he said. "One is that it challenges us all to think about music and the development of possible instruments, and the other, more important one is that we get a good piece."[14]

A San woman is pictured in Botswana. Ma heard Bushmen music during a visit to Africa's Kalahari Desert.

Chapter 6

BUSH, BACH, AND BLUEGRASS

Many things Ma had learned and experienced had stuck with him through the years. One item in particular ran across his mind on a regular basis: the lives of the Bushmen of the Kalahari Desert in Africa. Ever since he had first learned about them in an anthropology class, he had been left with a desire to travel to their native land, studying them up-close and personal. "I was fascinated by them. . . . So I thought to myself, one day I am going to go there."[1]

Into the Bush

That day finally came in 1993. With help from Professor DeVore, his anthropology professor from Harvard, Ma assembled a film crew and a guide/translator and set off for Bushman villages in the African nation of Namibia. He planned to make a documentary of the trip.

The Bushmen, also called the San, are a group of African people who have lived for centuries as hunters and gatherers. Their language is unique, as it features clicking sounds not heard in other languages. Many San still live in the traditional way, in small, mobile villages of about ten families that move around a large territory, gathering plants and fruit and hunting game. Other San, influenced by European culture, have settled into farming communities.

Ma brought his cello with him and played Bach for the Bushmen. They were not very interested. They wanted to play their music for him instead. Ma was fascinated by their homemade instruments, and he asked them many questions about how they worked. One instrument was made from the bows the Bushmen used to hunt. The player put the end of the bow in his mouth and hit the bowstring with his thumb and a stick. Another instrument, called the *gwashi*, was like a harp. It was made from natural materials, like wood, twigs, resin (tree sap), hide (dried animal skins), and sinew (strings made from animal tendons). Another instrument, called a *ventura*, is a little bit like a cello. It has one metal string, strung over an oil can. The bow is made from a twig. Ma tried to play the *ventura*, which he found difficult. He asked his translator to tell the Bushman *ventura* player he was much better at it.[2]

The high point of the trip for Ma was an ancient Bushman ritual called the trance dance. He described it as a ritual that was a combination of "music, medicine, [and] religion."[3] The women of the tribe sat around the fire, clapping and singing to a drumbeat, while the men danced, sometimes falling into a trance, or altered mental state.

Home Again

After returning from his Kalahari Desert trip, Ma had cut down his concert appearances to about seventy-five a year. Some of that newly freed time he spent at home, performing small domestic chores that made him feel part of family life. "I take great pride in taking dishes

The Meaning of Life

The day after he had witnessed the trance dance, Ma asked some of the San why they performed the ritual. They told him it was because it gives them meaning.

The entire trip brought new meaning to Ma's life and career. It redefined his concept of the musician's role in society. What he learned, he said, is that the purpose of a musician is "to uphold cultural memory, but also to innovate."[4] He decided that from then on, in addition to continuing his classical playing, he would try to learn and experiment with different kinds of music and cultures.

out of the dishwasher; in waking up my children to go to school; and I absolutely love grocery shopping," he has said.[5] To relax, he played chamber music with close friends who are amateur musicians.

Even with a reduced concert schedule, Ma was still spending about half of his nights away from home. While he was away, he thought about his family, and what his wife was going through as, essentially, a single parent. "She's really trying to do an incredible job in keeping us together," he told a reporter for *Strings* magazine in 1992. "I think, in a way, that's the center of my life. . . . It . . . gives me the strength to go out and do what I do."[6]

What he was doing at that point was making music, as well as making a film about his experiences in Africa. Even after Ma had completed the documentary, called *Distant Echoes*, what he had experienced in the Kalahari Desert stayed with him. "That was one of the most affecting trips or things that I've ever done in my life," said Ma. "There's hardly a week goes by I'm not thinking about that."[7]

Inspiration Strikes

It was during this period of renewed experimentation that Ma began what was to become the *Inspired by Bach* film project. In 1991, Ma received an invitation to approach Bach from a different perspective: as a speaker, not a performer. A friend asked him to speak at a meeting about Albert Schweitzer (1875–1965), a French musician, philosopher, and physician who was an expert

After a life-changing experience like visiting African Bushmen, Ma relishes the grounding influence and the support provided by his family. He is the first to acknowledge their role in his great success.

on Bach. Ma was going to talk about Schweitzer's essays on Bach.

After Ma reread Schweitzer's essays and gave his speech at the meeting, he began to get an idea of a new way to experience Bach's music. Schweitzer said Bach was a "painterly" or "pictorial" composer, meaning that his music created visual images in the minds of those listening to it. Ma decided to make films about Bach's cello suites, working with other creative artists who were not musicians. He wanted to see how nonmusicians would interpret the suites.[8] The project would be called *Inspired by Bach*.

Ma hoped that these films would be shown on television and bring Bach to a new audience.[9] He approached Rhombus Media, a Canadian production company, about producing the films. He chose them because they specialized in films about the performing arts. Rhombus thought it was a great idea. "Three minutes into the meeting, we said, 'Let's do it,'" head producer Niv Fichman recalled.[10] It would be years before the films were finished.

Many Modes of Musical Interpretation

Once production of the project got under way, Ma worked closely with Rhombus Media to choose different types of artists to interpret the cello suites for the camera. For the First Suite film, Ma picked Julie Moir Messervy, a garden designer. The Second Suite film explored the field of architecture in virtual reality through the drawings of Italian architect Giovanni Battista Piranesi. Born thirty-five years after Bach, Piranesi had created drawings of imaginary prisons so strange that they could not be built. The Third Suite film was based on an art form with close ties to music: dance. Ma chose modern dance choreographer, or dance creator, Mark Morris for the project. Called *Falling Down Stairs*, the Third Suite film was the first segment produced. Rhombus and Ma began filming it in summer 1994.

In the film series *Inspired by Bach*, Ma explored the great composer Johann Sebastian Bach from a new angle.

The Fourth Suite film was just that: a film. Directed by Canadian Atom Egoyan, it was the only one of the six Bach films that followed the outline of a fictional story, rather than a proper documentary. It followed several characters whose lives were linked by Bach's music. Ma appears as himself in the film. For the Fifth Suite film, Ma reached across the globe to Japan. He asked Kabuki actor Tamasaburo Bando to create a new Kabuki dance to the music. Kabuki is a traditional type of Japanese theater that features singing and dancing. The Sixth Suite film featured a different type of dancing—ice dancing. Jayne Torvill and Christopher Dean, the British ice-dancing champions, agreed to create a new routine to Bach's music.

Bumps Along the Way

Completing the Bach project was not easy. Some segments ran into problems. For the First Suite film, Ma and Messervy wanted to show a music garden in Boston that would reflect Bach's music. Different areas of the garden would represent different parts of the suite. People visiting the garden would be able to push a button to hear a recording of the music. Ma and Messervy met with many politicians in Boston to try to persuade them to build the garden in time for the film's deadline. The plan failed because no one would donate enough money to begin the project. Luckily, the city of Toronto offered to host the garden. Construction was barely begun in time for the film. Instead of showing the garden, most of the First Suite film documented Ma and Messervy's struggle to persuade Boston to build the garden. The film ends with a ribbon-cutting ceremony at the park-in-progress in Toronto.

The Fifth Suite film project almost stopped before it began. In June 1994, Ma was flying from the United States to Tokyo to meet with Tamasaburo, director Niv Fichman, and the rest of the documentary team. During a layover in the Detroit airport, Ma received some bad news from Fichman. The project was over. Only hours before Fichman was to begin filming, Tamasaburo had decided he did not want to do it. Ma was unwilling to give up. He went to Japan anyway. Once there, Ma managed to talk Tamasaburo into completing the film.[11]

Ma performed Bach's First Suite for Unaccompanied Cello at the opening of the Toronto Music Garden in 1999. The garden was constructed to reflect the suite's connection to nature.

New Music

Part of what Ma was doing was increasing his commitment to play new symphonic music. In 1994, he played works commissioned for him by American composers Christopher Rouse, John Harbison, Richard Danielpour, and sound track composer John Williams. That same year, Ma released a recording of twentieth-century music. It was called the *New York Album* because all the pieces were composed in New York. One of the pieces, by composer Stephen Albert, was a new cello concerto commissioned for Ma by the Baltimore Symphony. The CD won a 1994 Grammy Award for Best Instrumental Solo Performance (with orchestra).

Meanwhile, Ma was pursuing another musical experiment. In 1994, he began rehearsing with fiddler Mark O'Connor and bass player Edgar Meyer. Ma wanted to explore the fiddling style of stringed instrument

Back to Basics

During this period of experimentation with world and contemporary symphonic music, Ma also turned his attention back to the classical repertoire. He and Ax continued to collaborate on various chamber pieces. They played together at Tanglewood, and recorded three clarinet trios—one each by Brahms, Beethoven, and Mozart—with clarinetist Richard Stoltzman. The recording of the trios won a Grammy for Best Chamber Music Performance in 1995. It was Ma's tenth Grammy Award.

playing. Once the three men decided to work together, they began meeting about once a month to rehearse. It was difficult to coordinate their schedules, but they worked hard to find the time. "The rehearsals were very intense," said O'Connor. "Sometimes they would last more than 12 hours. We didn't have to do any of this, but we did it because we thought it mattered."[12]

It took a year for Ma to learn how to match O'Connor's and Meyer's style of playing, including their rhythmic precision and style of bowing. Ma even changed the way he held the bow while he was playing fiddle music. Eventually, he got the hang of it. "We came up with some really great fiddle material that we hoped would challenge him," said O'Connor. "It was amazing to see him process this intellectually and make it work on his instrument. It has been quite a transformation."[13]

The trio began touring to packed concert halls in 1995 and released an album called *Appalachia Waltz* in 1996. The tunes on the recording were composed or arranged by Meyer or O'Connor. The CD spent twenty weeks at the top of Billboard's Classical Crossover chart in 1997, remaining on the chart for more than a year and a half, and gained positive reviews. Ma was proving that his crossover projects could be both commercial and artistic successes.

Chapter 7

Even when Ma was playing well-known concertos with major orchestras, he still occasionally chose to do something a bit different. Most concertos are played in the first half of a concert, before intermission. After that, the soloist is usually finished for the night. But sometimes, instead of putting his cello away, Ma would sit in the back of the cello section and play in the orchestra for the second half of the concert. He particularly enjoyed doing this with the Philadelphia Orchestra. "It is an honor to play the back stands of the Philadelphia Orchestra," said Ma. "It's incredible the way those players listen, the knowledge they have. I admire it so much. And I feel the thrill of being part of something that's greater than the sum of its parts—being accepted as part of the team."[1]

In January 1996, Ma took center stage in an unusual concert series with the Philadelphia Orchestra. Most orchestra concerts contain only one concerto, and few orchestras plan concerts of only twentieth-century music. Ma and the Philadelphia Orchestra chose to defy both of those traditions. Ma played concerts made up entirely of three cello concertos written for him in the 1990s by Richard Danielpour, Leon Kirchner, and Christopher Rouse. Not long after the concerts, Ma recorded all three pieces with the orchestra during a huge blizzard that dumped three feet of snow on Philadelphia. The weather did not chill the recording. The CD went on to grab two Grammy Awards in 1997.

Ma and jazz trumpeter Wynton Marsalis teamed up to promote music education in 1997. Among his other achievements, Marsalis is well known for exposing young audiences to classical and jazz music.

Even though Ma was busy, he did not neglect music education. He continued to give master classes, and he even teamed up with trumpet player Wynton Marsalis to make a series of music-education videotapes. The four videotapes cover practicing, rhythm, musical forms, and jazz. A critic with the *Toronto Star* said Ma "steals the music-education series away from the motor-mouth trumpeter."[2] Ma has even occasionally visited public schools, as he did after a concert with the Baltimore Symphony in November 1997.

Flavor of Asia

As he traveled to many different countries, Yo-Yo Ma could not help noticing that musical traditions and

A Family of Musical Educators

Yo-Yo is not the only Ma to carry on the family tradition of promoting the music education that was so important to his father. His sister, Yeou-Cheng, is the executive director of the Children's Orchestra Society, founded by their father shortly after the family moved to New York City. The society runs four youth orchestras, a chamber music program, and private lessons for talented, motivated children. Yeou-Cheng juggles her responsibilities as executive director with her work as a pediatrician for the Albert Einstein College of Medicine in New York City, where she treats children with developmental disorders. She also continues to play the violin as a chamber musician.

Ma's sister and first recital partner, Yeou-Cheng, became a physician, but music has remained an important part of her life.

instruments seemed linked all over the world. In a museum in Japan, Ma saw a *biwa*—a pear-shaped stringed instrument—from the eighth century decorated with designs from Persia (modern-day Iran) and Central Asia. European stringed instruments such as the cello most likely have evolved from ancient Arabian and Chinese stringed instruments. By the mid-1990s, Ma was beginning to explore Asian, or "Eastern," music and how musical traditions in different geographic regions are linked.[3]

By 1997, Ma had become involved with several projects that explored traditional Chinese music. In his first major film project, Ma was featured on the sound track of the movie *Seven Years in Tibet*. The movie stars actor Brad Pitt as an Austrian mountain climber who journeys to Tibet during World War II. Although written by American composer John Williams, much of the music had an Eastern flavor.

Ma also collaborated with several composers of Chinese origin. In February 1997, Ma premiered *Spring Dreams*. It was written by Chinese-American composer Bright Sheng, a University of Michigan professor. Unlike most cello concertos, *Spring Dreams* was not written for a typical European/American orchestra. Instead, Ma was accompanied by the National Traditional Orchestra of China. Founded in 1960, the orchestra contains only traditional Chinese instruments. Although *Spring Dreams* was structured like a piece of Western classical music—in two movements—its melodies sounded very Chinese.

Ma's second collaboration with a Chinese composer took place in view of the entire world. He was a featured soloist in *Symphony 1997 (Heaven Earth Mankind)* by Tan Dun. The piece was commissioned to celebrate the return of Hong Kong to China after 150 years of British occupation. Dun wrote it for solo cello, Western-style orchestra, children's choir, and replicas of ancient Chinese bells. It was performed during the ceremony turning Hong Kong over to the Chinese, which was broadcast internationally. Sony Classical, Ma's record company, released a CD of the piece later that year.

In 1997, Hong Kong's sovereignty was returned to China at an elaborate ceremony. As England's Union Jack was lowered and the Chinese flag raised, Ma's solo could be heard.

Two to Tango

Ma's search for new kinds of music to play also took him to Buenos Aires, the capital of Argentina. He was investigating the tango, a dance form invented in Argentina. He was particularly interested in Argentinian composer Astor Piazzolla's compositions, wherein Piazzolla had taken traditional Argentine tango music and fused it with elements of classical music and jazz. Piazzolla's music was not always popular in Argentina because it was different from traditional tango. "Did you know that Astor Piazzolla got death threats?" Ma once asked. "People called and said: 'If you write another piece like that, you're dead.' I love that. Imagine people caring so much about music!"[4]

After months of reading Argentine books, studying Piazzolla's music, practicing, and rehearsing, Ma participated in two tango-related recordings, which were released in 1997. One was the sound track to a movie called *The Tango Lesson*, about a romance between a British film director and her Argentine tango instructor. Ma contributed a version of the Piazzolla piece "Libertango" to one track of the CD.

Ma also made a full-length CD of Piazzolla's music, called *Soul of the Tango*. He collaborated with some of the world's top tango players to make the recording. The CD featured a duet between Ma and Piazzolla playing the *bandoneon*, an Argentine accordion—even though Piazzolla died in 1992. Ma was playing along with a

Piazzolla recording from 1987. *Soul of the Tango* won the Grammy for Best Classical Crossover Album in 1998.

On December 4, 1997, Ma and an ensemble featuring piano, *bandoneon*, violin, guitar, and bass kicked off a tour of tango music in Seattle. The tour included appearances in Washington, DC, New York, and Baltimore. Later, Ma wrote the foreword to a book about Astor Piazzolla entitled *Le Grand Tango*.

A Great Performer

Meanwhile, Ma was still busy with other projects. In 1998, Lincoln Center in New York City featured Ma in its Great Performers series, sponsoring several concerts and events for him. Begun in 1965, the Great Performers series presents instrumentalists and vocalists who are at the top of their game, performing innovative music in creative ways. Ma showcased his tango skills in a Piazzolla concert. He also played two modern works for cello and orchestra: *Symphony 1997*, by Tan Dun, and *The Protecting Veil* by John Tavener. Later that year, Ma would play *The Protecting Veil* with the Los Angeles Chamber Orchestra and release a CD of the work, recorded with the Baltimore Symphony Orchestra.

The main focus of the Great Performers series was Ma's interpretations of the Bach cello suites. Lincoln Center screened the six *Inspired by Bach* films in March 1998, before their appearance on American public television in April 1998. Lincoln Center also sponsored a marathon concert of the cello suites at the Church of St. Ignatius Loyola in Manhattan. As he had in 1991 and several times since then, Ma performed all six Bach cello suites in one day. In the *New York Times*, critic James Oestreich praised the music and Ma's performance, saying, "The cello suites, in the hands of a master, can seem the grandest . . . of statements . . . Mr. Ma's technical command was complete, as usual. . . . This venture proved a notable success."[5]

The Reviews Are In

Ma's films of the Bach suites did not receive the same praise as his live performances of Bach's music. Critical reaction to the films was mixed. Most critics liked *Falling Down Stairs*, the film of the Third Suite featuring the Mark Morris Dance Troupe. Some critics praised the films featuring Kabuki and ice dancing (the Fifth and Sixth Suite films), but most thought the other films were "a more uneven lot," as one critic said.[6] Even Ma's friends were critical. One of his former college professors, Leon Kirchner, said the films were "baloney, unworthy of a supreme musician like Yo-Yo."[7]

Opinions were quite different about the new recording of all six Bach suites that Ma released along with the films. Critic Terry Teachout called them "a major musical achievement . . . a distinct improvement on the version he recorded at the age of 26."[8] Critic David Patrick Stearns wrote, "The recordings provide ample evidence that America's finest cellist is getting even better."[9]

Even with negative reviews of the *Inspired by Bach* films hitting the papers at the end of March 1998, Ma

Ma's 1998 recordings of Bach's *Six Suites for Unaccompanied Cello* were considered a triumph.

did not lose his sense of humor. On April 1, 1998, Ma told an interviewer for National Public Radio (NPR) he was going to give up the cello to play the *bandoneon*. NPR even aired a recording of Ma playing a movement of a cello suite on the Argentine instrument. Upset listeners called radio stations to complain about Ma's abandonment of his lifelong instrument. NPR and Ma had only one reply: "April Fool!" Those listeners had not realized that the report was just an April Fool's joke.[10]

At the same time, Ma had not stopped thinking about Bach. He had begun playing Bach's music differently. He was influenced by a growing movement within classical music to try to play pieces as they had been performed when they were written.[11] He began tuning his cello slightly lower when he played Bach. This was closer to the tuning of Bach's time. Ma held his bow a bit differently, too, with his hand higher up the stick. He was also influenced by what he had learned about fiddling by working with Mark O'Connor and Edgar Meyer on *Appalachia Waltz*. He felt that the fiddling style of playing was close to the music of Bach's time, called baroque.[12]

Fixing What's Baroque

Eventually, Ma decided he wanted to experiment more with playing Baroque music in a more authentic way. He decided he wanted to use a "period" instrument, which is an instrument built or changed to imitate the instruments of a certain time period. Ma chose to alter his Stradivarius cello—which was originally built during the Baroque period—to make it more closely resemble its original form. He removed the endpin, a metal post at the bottom of the cello that sticks into the floor. This forced him to grip the cello between his knees. He also changed his strings from modern metal to old-fashioned gut. Instrument makers in London and Paris flattened the bridge—the piece of carved, curved wood that holds up the strings—and changed the tailpiece, which anchors the strings at the base of the cello. These changes reduced the pressure on the body and neck of the instrument. Ma played the refitted cello with a Baroque bow, which is lighter and has a different curve from a modern bow. Players cannot play as loud using Baroque-style instruments and bows.

The initial transition was difficult, said Ma. "Gut strings are unreliable. . . . They squeak and squawk at times, and they constantly go out of tune. But what I learned is that with less volume, the experience is more private, more intimate. Playing with less tension encourages you to think, to reflect more. It's extremely pleasurable."[13]

Ma's first recording on the changed instrument, *Simply Baroque*, was released in January 1999. He made the recording with the Amsterdam Baroque Orchestra, which uses period instruments.

Not everyone enjoyed Ma's Baroque experiment as much as he did. Some critics did not think he was very good at playing cello in the Baroque style. After Ma played a concert in London in April 1999, critic Helen

Wallace of the London *Times* wrote, "There is more to playing a gut-strung cello with a Baroque bow than getting the equipment right." She criticized his tone, saying it sounded "squeezed," and said he did not play the notes in tune.[14]

Even though he received mixed reviews, Ma decided to leave his Stradivarius in its Baroque setup indefinitely. "The repertoire is so rich and beautiful, I want to continue to play it," he said.[15] He would record a sequel to his Baroque CD, called *Simply Baroque II*, the following year. The Bach cello suites were not included on either Baroque recording. Ma continued to play them on his Montagnana cello instead of the altered Stradivarius.

Old Friends, Young Students

Even with a variety of unusual projects making demands on his time, Ma was still able to deliver top-notch performances of standard cello concertos. His summer 1999 performance of concertos by Haydn and Schumann with the Chicago Symphony was very well received. A few months later, Ma could be found at his regular summer retreat: Tanglewood, one of his favorite places.

While there, Ma gave master classes and played chamber music with Emanuel Ax. He also played in *Don Quixote* with an orchestra of young American and German musicians.

Shortly after leaving Tanglewood, Ma flew to Weimar, Germany. He and the conductor of the Chicago Symphony, Daniel Barenboim, were starting a youth orchestra called the West-Eastern Divan Orchestra in hopes of encouraging peace in the Middle East. The one hundred student musicians in the group were from Middle Eastern countries such as Israel, Egypt, Syria, and Iraq.

Ma also worked with American young people— through television. In fall 1999, he appeared on the season opener of the hit animated children's program *Arthur* as a large, cello-playing gray rabbit with glasses. He and a hot young jazz saxophonist named Josh Redman performed in the episode, called "My Music Rules." The theme of the episode was that children should feel that it is okay to like more than one kind of music.

Chapter 8

LAUNCHING THE SILK ROAD PROJECT

Before there was an established sea route to transport goods between Asia and Europe, all such trade was conducted by land over what became known as the Silk Road. This network of trade routes wandered through Central Asia, connecting Mediterranean cities to China, Korea, and Japan. The original cargo that traveled along the route consisted mainly of silk, which is where it gets its name, as well as spices and other goods. Today, thanks to Yo-Yo Ma, the Silk Road now serves as a metaphoric highway bringing together Eastern and Western music, allowing for the exploration of how their traditions have influenced one another for hundreds of years.[1]

The Silk Road Ensemble performed at Carnegie Hall in 2005. This photo shows Ma playing with Jeffrey Beecher (background) on bass, Wu Man on pipa (center), and Malik Mansurov on tar (right).

Building the Road

Discussions concerning a project to bring Eastern and Western sounds together at some kind of musical crossroads began in 1998 between Ma and a few colleagues. The first step toward official creation of what Ma dubbed The Silk Road Project was the organization of a series of conferences outlining plans for the project. During a conference in Paris in June, Ma met Theodore Levin, an ethnomusicologist and professor at Dartmouth College. An ethnomusicologist studies music in relationship to culture. Levin had spent twenty-five years traveling in Central Asia and studying the region's traditional music. It was decided that Ma would be artistic director of the Silk Road Project—in charge of directing musical activities—and Levin would coordinate all of the project's other activities.

Ma had much bigger plans than just learning about shared musical history. He wanted to organize collaborations between Western (American and European) and Eastern (Asian) musicians that would result in new music based on multiple musical traditions. He also wanted to bring attention to the musical traditions of non-Western countries. He and Levin were concerned that some traditions could be lost as popular Western culture invaded more and more parts of the globe.

Sony Classical provided the initial funding to get the project started. Meanwhile, Levin and others traveled to Eastern Europe and Asia, seeking composers and musicians who would be willing and able to work with Westerners.

By 1999, Ma had assembled a panel to look at the work of forty composers from Central Asia and Eastern Asia. The panel chose sixteen composers to participate in the project and commissioned a new work from each of them. The composers' countries included Azerbaijan, Tajikistan, Uzbekistan, China, Mongolia, and Iran. Ma was also working to find additional funding for the project. One sponsor was the Aga Khan Trust for Culture, a nonprofit foundation dedicated to supporting traditional culture in Central Asia.

Asian Influence

Among the first activities of the Silk Road Project was an album by Ma of solo cello music. Most of the music on the CD reflects the influences of Eastern music. One piece, called *Seven Tunes Heard in China*, was composed by Bright Sheng.

In the fourth movement of Sheng's piece, titled "The Drunken Fisherman," Ma had to pluck and strum his strings instead of using the bow. Most of the time, cello players pluck the strings with the fingers or thumb of their right hand. Sheng's piece required a different technique. The tune was originally performed in China on a seven-stringed plucked instrument like a guitar. To make the cello sound more like a guitar, Ma needed a pick. He decided to use the key card from his hotel room as a pick after discovering that it created the perfect sound.

All these projects kept Ma very busy, and busy people can sometimes be forgetful. In October 1999, Ma made headlines when he accidentally left his Montagnana cello in a New York taxicab. He was on his way to his hotel after visiting Isaac Stern, and planned to meet his wife to take her to dinner. Ma was a little surprised by how much press attention this received. He said, "I can play concerts for years and years and years, and you know, some people will say, 'How very nice. Nice playing. Thank you very much.' But you lose one cello in a taxicab, everybody knows about it! [They give you] the knowing look: 'Oh. Hi. Been in a taxi lately?'"[2]

Luckily, Ma had saved his cab receipt. Police were able to track down the cab and driver in only a few hours. The cab was in a garage in Queens, New York. The cab driver did not even realize the $2.5 million cello was still in his trunk. Ma was very relieved to get the priceless instrument back. "Somehow magic happened, and I have my cello," he said. "The instrument is my voice, so I need it. . . . [Otherwise] I would be crying right now."[3]

Taking Silk Road on the Road

By summer 2000, the Silk Road Project was ready to begin the next step: preparing for performance. Ma organized a twelve-day workshop at Tanglewood. He and Levin invited about sixty musicians from all over the world to meet there and rehearse. The group became known as the Silk Road Ensemble. They were trying out the new pieces of music that had been composed for the project. With so many different countries represented, the musicians had to have translators so they could talk to each other. Most of the musicians were from countries such as Mongolia, China, and Iran—although some already made their homes in the United States—but some were Americans or Europeans trained in classical music. Like Ma himself, these classical players were eager to experiment with playing Eastern-style music.[4]

For his part, Ma did not stop at playing Silk Road–inspired pieces on his cello. He learned to play a new instrument, the *morin khuur*, also called the Mongolian horse-head fiddle. The top of the neck of the instrument, called the scroll, is carved like a horse's head. It has two

Ma played the *morin khuur* in rehearsals with the Silk Road Ensemble in 2003 in Toronto, Canada.

strings. One of the reasons Ma was interested in the fiddle is that his family name, Ma, means "horse." Ma felt that the style of playing used for the horse-head fiddle was similar to Baroque cello and Western fiddle playing. "Take away all the technological developments," Ma said, "and you find the point, maybe 500 years ago, where all the musical traditions converse with each other."[5]

Ma's involvement with the Silk Road Project also led him to another film project. He played on the sound track of the movie *Crouching Tiger, Hidden Dragon*, directed by Ang Lee. The score, by composer Tan Dun, was written for a Western orchestra and Asian instruments. Dun was trying to make music that sounded like a blend

Yo-Yo Ma and violinist Itzhak Pearlman performed a selection of Best Song nominations at the 73rd Annual Academy Awards at the Shrine Auditorium in Los Angeles in 2001.

of Western and Eastern musical traditions.[6] To get a feel for the music, Ma watched scenes from the movie. He recorded his part without hearing the accompanying orchestra parts. The sound track was nominated for an Oscar and won for Best Original Score. Ma performed excerpts at the Oscar ceremony.

The More the Merrier

At the beginning of 2001, the Silk Road Project expanded its efforts to include more music and more countries. A panel reviewed the work of composers from Armenia, Italy, India, Japan, Korea, Pakistan, and Turkey. They picked four more composers to create new musical

Taking a Break From the "Road"

Ma's new commitment to exploring Central and East Asian music did not stop him from continuing to dedicate time to education. In June 2000, he was a guest artist at the World Cello Congress held at Towson University outside Baltimore, Maryland. He gave several master classes, including one for very young cellists.

In December 2000, he and Emanuel Ax reunited for a duo tour to celebrate their twenty-fifth year of playing together. Ma, Edgar Meyer, and Mark O'Connor also teamed with bluegrass singer Alison Krauss and singer-songwriter James Taylor to record the Grammy-winning album *Appalachian Journey*. Near Christmas 2000, Ma tried out a new career: acting. He appeared as himself on an episode of the popular television drama *The West Wing*.

works. The Silk Road Ensemble was scheduled to begin performances in August 2001.

Just before leaving for their tour, the Ensemble gathered in France for a week of rehearsals. Ma was pleased with how well the group worked together. "What's impressive about this group is that there are so many leaders, so many people who can take charge," said Ma. "Everybody takes a leadership role in something. None of us knows everything about everything, but when we pool our resources we have a pretty incredible knowledge base."[7]

The musicians in the ensemble were just as pleased with Ma. Kayhan Kalhor said, "As I've gotten to know Yo-Yo, I've come to admire not only his energetic, charismatic musicianship but his character. He creates this positive energy wherever he is, and that's a rare person, anywhere."[8]

The Silk Road Project's 2001–2002 tour was planned in cooperation with partner cities. Each city hosted a multiday festival of performances, lectures, and workshops. The first Partner City Festival took place at the Schleswig-Holstein Music Festival in Germany. The weeklong festival showcased the new music that had been commissioned for the Silk Road Project, as well as traditional music from Central and East Asia, performed on traditional instruments. Each concert also featured a piece of "standard" classical music that had been influenced by Eastern music. Each of the Silk

Road Ensemble's concerts throughout its tour would follow this format.

Audiences and critics alike were fascinated. "In one Silk Road concert in Germany I worried about whether I had given enough information in introducing a singer from a very different cultural background," said Ma. "But the audience just burst into wild applause at the end, and I didn't really need to explain anything."[9]

Touched by Asia

During Ma's fourth year of directing the Silk Road Project, he agreed to stay on for another four years. Dr. Levin chose to step down from his post of curatorial director and offer his assistance as curatorial consultant. The Silk Road Project soon announced its 2002–2003

On the Record

No musical endeavor by Yo-Yo Ma would be complete without a recording. In 2002, Sony Classical released the first album featuring the Silk Road Ensemble. It is called *Silk Road Journeys: When Strangers Meet*. It contains traditional Mongolian, Persian, and Chinese music, as well as compositions by numerous Silk Road Project participants.

Other Silk Road recordings include *Silk Road Journeys: Beyond the Horizon* (2005), *New Impossibilities* (2007), *Traditions and Transformations: Sounds of the Silk Road Chicago* (2008), *Off the Map* (2009), and *A Playlist Without Borders* (2013).

tour schedule, which included Chicago and Las Vegas, and cities in Italy, California, Vancouver, and Toronto.

By this point, the Silk Road Project was influencing Ma's solo career as well. Many of his appearances with major symphony orchestras featured music inspired by the Silk Road Project. In February 2003, Ma premiered a piece by Tan Dun called *The Map*. It was written for cello and orchestra, accompanied by visual multimedia. The piece was a hit with the audience at its premiere with the Boston Symphony Orchestra.

In late April and early May of 2003, the Silk Road Ensemble finally traveled to Central Asia to give master classes and performances in the countries of Kazakhstan, Kyrgyzstan, and Tajikistan. The Ensemble performed in spots along the actual Silk Road.

The Road to Education

In 2009, Ma created an educational initiative called Silk Road Connect. The program is basically a partnership with schools to increase participation in the arts. The Silk Road Project supports a school's team of teachers, who come from many different disciplines or subjects, by providing lesson plans and materials. Lesson plans include *Along the Silk Road*, which teaches middle and high school students about the many ways that the original Silk Road connected East Asia and the Mediterranean. This plan was developed in conjunction with Stanford University's Program on International and Cross-Cultural Education.

Ma was the cello soloist in Tan Dun's, "The Map," a musical piece accompanied by visual media, which he performed with the Boston Symphony Orchestra at Boston's Symphony Hall in 2003.

Also available to teachers is a guide titled *Silk Road Encounters*. The guide offers classroom materials, activity plans, and references for those teaching students about the Silk Road.

In addition to lesson plans and material, the Silk Road Project provides hands-on activities in the arts. Members of the Silk Road Ensemble and various performing artists from each local community visit schools to speak and lead arts activities.[10]

Additionally, the organization has established agreements with Harvard University—Ma's alma mater—and the Rhode Island School of Design to establish residency programs on their campuses. A residency is when teachers and artists remain at a school for a certain length of time in order to share their knowledge and experiences. Members of the Silk Road Ensemble typically taught courses, lead workshops, and performed at these schools as part of their residencies. The School of Design residency program ran for five years, from 2005 to 2010. Harvard's long-term partnership with the Silk Road Project had residencies ongoing until 2015.[11] Other US and international universities have benefitted from shorter residencies by ensemble members.

Chapter 9

Remarkably, even while trying to juggle his performing career with his duties as artistic director of the Silk Road Project, Ma still found time to explore different kinds of music. In April 2003, he released a recording that explored his cultural roots: not Chinese, but French.

"French music was in my earliest memories," Ma explained. "It's so in my blood. . . . It's what soul food is for some people."[1]

The CD, called *Paris: La Belle Époque*, features four works by French composers written around the turn of the twentieth century. None of the pieces were originally written for cello. Instead, they are pieces for violin and piano. One, the sonata by César Franck, has been played by cellists for decades. Ma arranged the other three pieces himself for cello and piano. He made the recording with friend and longtime recital partner Kathryn Stott. The two toured together during winter and spring 2003, performing pieces from the recording as well as other selections by composers from France, Russia, and Argentina.

Ma soon followed up his musical trip to France with an album dedicated to the music of Brazil, called *Obrigado Brazil*. The CD hit stores in July 2003. In February 2004, it was awarded a Grammy for Best Classical Crossover Album.

Ma's interest in Brazilian music was piqued when he was in South America working on his Piazzolla project. Ma had kept in touch with a guitarist from the project, Oscar Castro-Neves. The two wanted to work together again, so Ma began listening to as much Brazilian music as he could. The initial collaboration between the men swelled into an ensemble that included internationally acclaimed guitarists Sérgio and Odair Assad, vocalist Rosa Passos, pianist Kathryn Stott, and several others. The group toured over the summer and fall of 2003 in support of an album of their music, including a stop in Tanglewood in July.

Ambassador Ma

Ma's efforts toward making connections between students and the arts caught the attention of many influential people. In 2001, the United States Department of State named him one of its CultureConnect ambassadors. The CultureConnect program sends performing artists, writers, architects, and athletes to countries around the world to share their time and talents with young people. Ambassadors conduct master classes, perform, lead discussions, and act as mentors. Among the activities Ma has taken part in through the program were performing as guest soloist in 2003 for a concert by members of the United States' National Symphony Orchestra and the Iraq National Symphony in Washington, DC. Ma has taught master classes and performed in several countries as well, including trips to Lebanon, Korea, Lithuania, and China.

In 2006, the United Nations also tapped into Ma's desire to build bridges through music and the arts by naming him a Messenger of Peace. These official representatives are meant to promote the mission of the UN—namely, peace and cooperation among the world's nations and people. Ma was made a Messenger of Peace because of his efforts to overcome cultural differences through the Silk Road Project and other artistic means. "Through your music, the message of peace can spread far and wide and influence people around the world to focus on harmony and human dignity," said Kofi Anan, who was then Secretary-General of the UN, when he nominated Ma for the position.[2]

In 2008, Ma decided it was time to experiment (again) with not only how he made music, but how it was recorded. Upon the release of his album *Songs of Joy & Peace* that year, he posted a recording of himself playing *Dona Nobis Pacem* (*Bring Us Peace*) on the Internet and invited amateur musicians to add tracks—thereby virtually playing with Yo-Yo Ma. He and representatives of social networking company Indaba Music would listen to submissions and pick a winner, who would then have the opportunity to record with Ma for real in the studio.[3]

Presidents and Politicians

Ma began 2009 with a very high-profile performance: playing at the inauguration of US President Barack Obama. He was joined on a very chilly outdoor stage by violinist Itzhak Pearlman, pianist Gabriela Montero, and clarinetist Anthony McGill. This special quartet played a piece that was written specifically for the event, composer John Williams's "Air and Simple Gifts." News outlets reported that this appearance marked the first time that a classical quartet had been chosen to perform at a US presidential inauguration.

There was a lot of talk about how the music audiences heard did not quite match-up with the movements of the musicians on stage. It was later revealed that the quartet had pre-recorded the piece two days earlier. Although Ma and the others actually did play that day, most people heard the pre-recorded version of Williams's composition, which was piped through loudspeakers. The reason for this bit of recording magic was that the extreme cold on the day of the inauguration would cause the instruments to go out of tune quickly. The result would sound horrible. Ma and his fellow musicians felt it was better not to risk ruining this special occasion with

Itzhak Perlman, Ma, and Anthony McGill are shown performing during Barack Obama's inauguration as the 44th US President on January 20, 2009, in Washington, DC.

sour music, and used the recorded version as insurance against that happening.[4]

In the summer of that same year, Ma had the sad honor of playing at the funeral of Senator Edward Kennedy. Senator Kennedy was the younger brother of the late President John F. Kennedy, who was present at Ma's American debut as a cellist. For this somber occasion, Ma returned to one of his favorite works, playing the Sarabande movement (which is played at a slow tempo) from Bach's Sixth Cello Suite. He also performed Franck's *Panis Angelicus*, sung by operatic tenor Placido Domingo.

Slide Show, With Music

Even as he played more traditional concerts, Ma continued to experiment with new forms of art and performance. A May 2009 concert at the American Museum of Natural History in New York City featured the premiere of a contemporary piece for cello and percussion titled "Self Comes to Mind." The composer, Bruce Adolphe, created a musical interpretation of how a human brain becomes a mind, capable of thought and reasoning. Ma's performance, with percussionists John Ferrari and Ayano Kataoka, was accompanied by full-color brain scans and other images flashing on a screen in time with the music.[5]

The end of the year brought a much happier event for Ma and all concerned. On Nov. 3, 2009, Ma was appointed to the President's Committee on the Arts and Humanities. This committee advises the US White House on matters having to do with arts and culture. Ma was chosen, in part, because he was quite familiar with two areas on which the committee focuses: arts education and cultural exchange.[6]

Band of Citizens

The following month, the Chicago Symphony Orchestra (CSO) received funds from two generous donors to create a new artistic position with the organization. The Judson and Joyce Green creative consultant would serve as a kind of outreach coordinator for education

Ma has performed at the funerals of several dignitaries, including the service honoring *The Washington Post* publisher Katharine Graham.

programs. Because of his reputation not only as a world-class instrumentalist, but as a strong proponent of music education, Ma was named to fill the post.

He began to make his mark with the program beginning in 2010, when he started a project called Citizen Musician. The idea behind this program was to make music available, and enjoyable, to everyone in the greater Chicago area. Ma tried to recruit professional and amateur musicians, as well as music lovers of all kinds, to share their skills and appreciation with others in the community.[7]

Essentially, the program helps people of all ages, races, and life situations tell their personal stories through music. This was to be accomplished by bringing music anyplace and every place: the program has held workshops and performances in locations as varied as school classrooms and prisons. Citizen Musicians also have been responsible for impromptu performances, such as a 2011 "flash mob" by the Chicago Children's Choir in a Chicago train station and a "pop-up" concert by the Chicago Civic Orchestra in a downtown shopping center.[8]

China Exchange and US Honors

For four days in November of 2011, Ma joined actress Meryl Streep, author Amy Tan, film director Joel Cohen, and other American artists and performers in Beijing, China, as part of a program called the US-China Forum on the Arts and Culture. The project was part of an agreement regarding culture exchanges signed by both nations in 2010. Actors, musicians, artists, and others from both countries met to discuss their works and perform for each other and the public.[9] The event was organized by the Asia Society and the Aspen Institute in the United States and the China People's Association for Friendship with Foreign Countries, which is a department of the Chinese government's Ministry of Foreign Affairs.

Beijing was the first meeting of the forum. True to his desire to have other artists interpret his music, Ma performed with American urban "street" dancer Charles "Lil' Buck" Riley. The two reportedly did not rehearse their performance, but chose instead to improvise, and they made it up as they went along.[10]

Nine months earlier, Ma had been awarded the Presidential Medal of Freedom by US President Barack Obama. The award, which is the highest civilian honor in the United States, is presented to those who have contributed greatly to society in matters of culture, national interests, or world peace. Shortly after his trip to China, he and his US-China Forum "teammate" Streep were honored, with others, by the Kennedy Center for the Performing Arts for their lifelong achievements in the arts. The Kennedy Center Honors have been likened to getting a knighthood in Great Britain.[11]

Goat Rodeo Sessions

Between 2012 and 2014, Ma was the recipient of a number of awards, including another Grammy for an album titled *The Goat Rodeo Sessions*. A "goat rodeo" is a slang

President Barack Obama awarded the 2010 Medal of Freedom to Ma during a ceremony at the White House.

term used to describe a situation that is full of energy but, because so many people and ideas are involved, it is difficult to make everything turn out all right. In this instance, Ma and bluegrass musicians Stuart Duncan, Edgar Meyer, and Chris Thile were trying to combine classical and bluegrass music, which could be difficult. Apparently the quartet succeeded, though, as evidenced by the album's Grammy win for Best Folk Album.

Among the awards he received during this time frame, he was particularly honored to have been the inaugural, or first, winner of the Fred Rogers Legacy Award in 2014. Fred Rogers was better known as Mister Rogers, of *Mister Rogers' Neighborhood*. Through his work on that television program, Rogers was able to teach young children valuable lessons in pride, creativity, kindness—all the things that make someone a good, well-rounded human being. The award named for him honors someone who has acted according to the values that Rogers held and shared.

Ma had appeared on *Mister Rogers' Neighborhood*, and he and Rogers became friends. Rogers' wife, Joanne, chose Ma to be the first recipient of the award because of his work with children, providing music education on many levels.

Upon being given the award, Ma said, "This is perhaps the greatest honor I've ever received."[12]

The award ceremony and recital afterward raised $1 million for the center. During the recital, Ma played a wide selection of tunes, including an Appalachian waltz, a Mongolian folk tune, and one of Rogers' favorite classical hymns. Ma added one of his favorites, Bach's Cello Suite No. 1, to the program. He said the upbeat third movement of the piece showed how thrilled and excited he was about receiving the award.[13]

A Musical Explorer for the Ages

For Ma, music is about communication. He believes music can bring people together, and that exploring music of other cultures is a way to overcome national boundaries.[14]

"Everything that I've experienced as a cellist, as a travelling musician, as an immigrant, as a tricultural person has made me think about cultural connections," he told a reporter for London's *The Guardian* newspaper in 2015.[15]

So what kind of music will Yo-Yo Ma be playing in a few years? He may not even know himself. One thing is certain: Ma is likely to remain not only the world's foremost cellist but also its most enthusiastic musical explorer. "Being artistic," he says, "is going to the edge and then reporting back."[16]

Chronology

1955—Yo-Yo Ma is born in Paris, France, on October 7.

1959—Begins studying cello with his father.

1962—Ma family moves to New York City.

1964—Enters the Pre-College Division of the Juilliard School; begins studying with faculty member Leonard Rose.

1968—Receives excellent reviews for performance of Saint-Saëns cello concerto with the San Francisco Little Symphony.

1971—Gives recital in New York's Carnegie Hall on May 6; graduates from Professional Children's School in June at age fifteen.

1972—Enters Harvard University.

1976—Graduates from Harvard with a bachelor of arts in humanities.

1978—Marries Jill Hornor; wins Avery Fisher Prize.

1980—Undergoes successful operation to correct curvature of the spine.

1983—Purchases cello made in 1733 by Italian maker Domenico Montagnana; first child, Nicholas, is born.

1984—Wins first Grammy Award, for recording of Bach cello suites; acquires Davidoff Stradivarius cello; principal cello teacher, Leonard Rose, dies.

1985—Daughter, Emily, is born; wins two Grammy Awards.

1986—Recording of Beethoven Cello Sonata No. 4 with Emanuel Ax wins Grammy for Best Chamber Music Performance.

1991—Plays concert of all six Bach suites in New York; receives honorary doctorate from Harvard University; plays "Begin Again Again" by Tod Machover on hypercello; father dies on August 28.

1992—Records best-selling album *Hush* with vocalist Bobby McFerrin.

1993—Visits Bushmen in Kalahari Desert in Africa; films documentary of trip called *Distant Echoes*.

1996—Releases best-selling album *Appalachia Waltz* with Edgar Meyer and Mark O'Connor.

1997—Featured on sound track of movie *Seven Years in Tibet*.

1998—*Soul of the Tango* wins Grammy for Best Classical Crossover Album; *Inspired by Bach* films shown on PBS; founds Silk Road Project.

1999—Releases *Solo*, album of solo cello music drawn from Silk Road Project; grabs headlines after leaving Montagnana cello in New York taxicab.

2000—Plays on Grammy-winning soundtrack for *Crouching Tiger, Hidden Dragon*; *Appalachian Journey* gains Ma his fourteenth Grammy Award.

2001—Silk Road Project begins Partner City Festival tour.

2002—Releases *Silk Road Journeys: When Strangers Meet*, first album featuring Silk Road Ensemble, and *Yo-Yo Ma Plays the Music of John Williams*.

2003—Releases two recordings, *Paris: La Belle Époque* and *Obrigado Brazil*.

2004—Wins Grammy for Best Classical Crossover Album for *Obrigado Brazil*.

2005—Receives an honorary degree, Doctor of Musical Arts, from Princeton University; releases first album with Silk Road Ensemble, *Beyond the Horizon*.

2006—Named United Nations Messenger of Peace; cofounds pro-Asian Committee of 100.

2009—Plays at the inauguration of President Barack Obama and the funeral of Senator Edward Kennedy; appointed to the President's Committee on the Arts and Humanities; receives a Grammy Award for *Songs of Joy & Peace*.

2010—Named Judson and Joyce Green creative consultant for the Chicago Symphony Orchestra, and launches Citizen Musician program; plays on the sound track for the documentary *Jews and Baseball: An American Love Story*.

2011—Receives Kennedy Center Honors recognition and the Presidential Medal of Freedom.

2012—Receives the Grammy Award for Best Folk Album for *The Goat Rodeo Sessions*.

2013—Performs at a service for the Boston Marathon bombing victims.

2014—Receives the inaugural Fred Rogers Legacy Award.

2015—Releases *Songs from the Arc of Life*; undertakes a tour of Asia with his collaborator on that album, pianist Kathryn Stott; the documentary *The Music of Strangers: Yo-Yo Ma and the Silk Road Ensemble* premieres at the Toronto (Canada) International Film Festival.

Chapter Notes

CHAPTER 1. SHARING THE "SUITE" LIFE

1. Richard Dyer, "Crossing Over: Yo-Yo Ma Makes Collaborative Music Films Out of Bach's Solo Cello Suites," *Boston Globe*, March 29, 1998, p. N1.

2. Bonnie Churchill, "'Inspired' Idea: Cellist Yo-Yo Ma Hopes to Widen the Audience for Classical Music With a Unique PBS Collaboration," *Boston Herald*, March 29, 1998, p. O41.

3. Walter Goodman, "Television Review; Cellist Finds Accompanists for J.S. Bach," *New York Times*, April 1, 1998, http://www.nytimes.com/1998/04/01/arts/television-review-cellist-finds-accompanists-for-j-s-bach.html.

4. Edith Eisler, "Continuity in Diversity," *Strings*, May/June 2001, p. 51.

CHAPTER 2. THE BIGGER, THE BETTER

1. Janet Tassel, "Yo-Yo Ma's Journeys," *Harvard Magazine*, March–April 2000, http://www.harvard-magazine. com/issues/ma00/yoyoma.html (March 2, 2003).

2. Marina Ma and John A. Rallo, *My Son, Yo-Yo* (Hong Kong: The Chinese University Press, 1995), p. 29.

3. Krista Tippett, et al., "Transcript for Yo-Yo Ma: Music Happens Between the Notes," *On Being*, posted Sept. 2014, retrieved Nov. 2015, http://www.onbeing.org/program/yo-yo-ma-music-happens-between-the-notes/transcript/6733.

4. David Blum, "Ma Energetico," *Strad*, January 1988, p. 21.

5. Amelia Pang. "This Is New York: The Untold Story of Dr. Yeou-Cheng Ma, Violin Prodigy and Medical Doctor," *Epoch Times*, posted Aug. 2014, retrieved Nov. 2015, http://www.theepochtimes.com/n3/830952-this-is-new-york-the-untold-story-of-dr-yeou-cheng-ma-violin-prodigy-and-medical-doctor/.

6. David Blum, "A Process Larger Than Oneself," *New Yorker*, May 1, 1989, pp. 41–74. Reprinted in Blum, David. *Quintet: Five Journeys Toward Musical Fulfillment* (Ithaca NY: Cornell University Press, 1998), p. 8.

7. Pang.

8. Gale Research, *Contemporary Musicians*, Volume 2 (Farmington Hills, MI.: The Gale Group, 1989). Reproduced in *Biography Resource Center*, 2002, http://galenet.galegroup. com/servlet/BioRC (May 8, 2002).

9. Ma and Rallo, p. 63.

10. Blum, *Strad*, p. 21.

11. YouTube, "Leonard Bernstein Presents 7-Year-Old Yo-Yo Ma's High-Profile Debut for President John F. Kennedy," https://www.youtube.com/watch?v=dNvAUobb1y4.

12. Ibid.

13. Blum, *Quintet: Five Journeys Toward Musical Fulfillment*, p. 10.

14. Robert Sherman, "Celebrities Help École Française," *New York Times*, December 18, 1964.

15. Blum, *Quintet: Five Journeys Toward Musical Fulfillment*, p. 10.

16. Ibid., p. 10.

17. Ma and Rallo, pp. 101–104.

18. Blum, *Quintet: Five Journeys Toward Musical Fulfillment*, p. 10.

19. Richard Thorne, "The Magic of Yo-Yo Ma," *Saturday Review*, July 1981, p. 56.

20. Ma and Rallo, pp. 97–98.

CHAPTER 3. LESSONS LEARNED

1. Lloyd Schwartz, "On Tour with Yo-Yo Ma," *Harvard Magazine*, January–February 1982, p. 38.

2. Ed Siegel, "Playing the Full Human Range," *Boston Globe*, August 6, 1995, p. B29.

3. Susan Elliott, "Ax & Ma: Duo Extraordinary," *Musical America*, May 1990, p. 23.

4. Richard Thorne, "The Magic of Yo-Yo Ma," *Saturday Review*, July 1981, p. 56.

5. Janet Tassel, "Yo-Yo Ma's Journeys," *Harvard Magazine*, March–April 2000, http://www.harvard-magazine. com/issues/ma00/yoyoma.html (March 2, 2003).

6. Marina Ma and John A. Rallo, *My Son, Yo-Yo* (Hong Kong: The Chinese University Press, 1995), pp. 124–128.

7. Edith Eisler, "Yo-Yo Ma: Music from the Soul," *Strings*, May/June 1992, p. 50.

8. Anne Inglis, "In Pursuit of Excellence," *Strad*, May 1984, p. 30.

9. Tassel.

10. Herbert Kupferberg, "Yo-Yo Ma," *Stereo Review*, April 1990, p. 71.

11. Tassel.

12. Ibid.

13. David Blum, "A Process Larger Than Oneself," *New Yorker*, May 1, 1989, pp. 41–74. Reprinted in Blum, David. *Quintet: Five Journeys Toward Musical Fulfillment* (Ithaca: NY: Cornell University Press, 1998), p. 14.

14. Ibid.

15. Tassel.

16. Schwartz, p. 38.

17. Ibid., p. 39.

18. Ibid., p. 38.

CHAPTER 4. THE START OF SOMETHING BIG

1. Lloyd Schwartz, "On Tour with Yo-Yo Ma," *Harvard Magazine*, January–February 1982, p. 40.

2. Richard Dyer, "Classical Music: With Ear for Diversity, Cellist Yo-Yo Ma Has the World on a String," *Boston Globe*, June 22, 2003, p. N6.

3. Janet Tassel, "Yo-Yo Ma's Journeys," *Harvard Magazine*, March–April 2000, http://www.harvard-magazine. com/issues/ma00/yoyoma.html (March 2, 2003).

4. David Blum, "A Process Larger Than Oneself," *New Yorker*, May 1, 1989, pp. 41–74. Reprinted in Blum, David. *Quintet: Five Journeys Toward Musical Fulfillment* (Ithaca NY: Cornell University Press, 1998), p. 18.

5. Ibid., p. 19.

6. Ibid., p. 20.

7. Joseph Horowitz, "Yo-Yo Ma Plays Cello," *New York Times*, April 17, 1978, p. C19.

8. Herbert Kupferberg, "Yo-Yo Ma," *Stereo Review*, April 1990, p. 72.

9. Heidi Waleson, "Two Soloists Make a Different Kind of Duo," *New York Times*, November 20, 1988, p. 27.

10. Richard Thorne, "The Magic of Yo-Yo Ma," *Saturday Review*, July 1981, p. 58.

11. Blum, p. 21.

12. Schwartz, p. 35.

13. Ibid, p. 38.

14. "Yo-Yo's Way With the Strings," *Time*, January 19, 1981, p. 55.

15. Thorne, p. 58.

16. Blum, p. 20.

17. Schwartz, p. 40.

18. Tim Page, "Leonard Rose Benefit," *New York Times*, November 1, 1986, p. 11.

CHAPTER 5. PUSHING MUSICAL BOUNDARIES

1. David Blum, "A Process Larger Than Oneself," *New Yorker*, May 1, 1989, pp. 41–74. Reprinted in Blum, David. *Quintet: Five Journeys Toward Musical Fulfillment* (Ithaca NY: Cornell University Press, 1998), p. 20.

2. Edith Eisler, "Yo-Yo Ma: Music From the Soul," *Strings*, May/June 1992, p. 50.

3. Ed Siegel, "Playing the Full Human Range," *Boston Globe*, August 6, 1995, p. B29.

4. Committee of 100. "About Us." Retrieved Dec. 2015, http://www.committee100.org/aboutus/aboutus.htm.

5. Bernard Holland, "Ma and Ax Perform Bolcom," *New York Times*, May 8, 1990, p. 19.

6. Susan Elliott, "Ax & Ma: Duo Extraordinary," *Musical America*, May 1990, p. 24.

7. Richard Dyer, "Ma and McFerrin: A Match Made in Tanglewood," *Boston Globe*, January 19, 1991, p. 18.

8. Eisler, p. 51.

9. Blum, p. 33.

10. Eisler, pp. 52–53.

11. Ibid., p. 53.

12. Ibid., p. 54.

13. Philip Kennicott, "A Born Idealist," *Gramophone*, April 1996, p. 17.

14. Eisler, p. 52.

CHAPTER 6. BUSH, BACH, AND BLUEGRASS

1. Philip Kennicott, "A Born Idealist," *Gramophone*, April 1996, p. 16.

2. Janet Tassel, "Yo-Yo Ma's Journeys," *Harvard Magazine*, March–April 2000, http://www.harvard-magazine. com/issues/ma00/yoyoma.html (March 2, 2003).

3. Kennicott, p. 16.

4. Matthew Gurewitsch and Philip Herrera, "Master Ma," *Town & Country*, February 1998, pp. 47ff.

5. Tan Shzr Ee, "Snake? It's OK, Take Me to the Desert," *Straits Times* (Singapore), March 12, 1999, pp. 1, L3.

6. Phan Ming Yen, "Yo-Yo Ma's Whirlwind Schedule," *Straits Times* (Singapore), November 18, 1993, pp. 1, L2, L4.

7. Beverly Schuch, "Internationally Known Cellist Yo-Yo Ma Continues to Expand His Musical Horizons," *CNN Pinnacle*, August 4, 2001 (transcript).

8. Richard Dyer, "Crossing Over: Yo-Yo Ma Makes Collaborative Music Films Out of Bach's Solo Cello Suites," *Boston Globe*, March 29, 1998, p. N1.

9. Bonnie Churchill, "'Inspired' Idea; Cellist Yo-Yo Ma Hopes to Widen the Audience for Classical Music with a Unique PBS Collaboration," *Boston Herald*, March 29, 1998, p. O41.

10. Mitch Potter, "Inspired by Bach," *Toronto Star*, October 18, 1997, p. J1.

11. Peter Goddard, "Yo-Yo Ma," *Toronto Star*, January 6, 1996, p. K1.

12. David Balakrishnan, "String Players' Waltz," *Strings*, March/April 1997, p. 34.

13. Jamie James, "Yo-Yo Ma May Be a National Institution, But He Continues to Reinvent Himself," *New York Times*, December 31, 1995.

CHAPTER 7. A WORLD OF MUSIC

1. Matthew Gurewitsch and Philip Herrera, "Master Ma," *Town & Country*, February 1998, pp. 47ff.

2. Peter Goddard, "Yo-Yo Ma," *Toronto Star*, January 6, 1996, p. K1.

3. Jamie James, "Yo-Yo Ma May Be a National Institution, But He Continues to Reinvent Himself," *New York Times*, December 31, 1995.

4. Justin Davidson, "Have Cello, Will Travel," *Newsday*, November 30, 1997, p. D10.

5. James R. Oestreich, "Bach's Life in Six Suites as Presented by Yo-Yo Ma," *New York Times*, March 16, 1998.

6. Richard Dyer, "As TV, Bach Films' Reach Exceeds Their Grasp," *Boston Globe*, March 29, 1998, p. N4.

7. Janet Tassel, "Yo-Yo Ma's Journeys," *Harvard Magazine*, March–April 2000, http://www.harvard-magazine. com/issues/ma00/yoyoma.html (March 2, 2003).

8. Terry Teachout, "At the Top of His Powers," *Time*, March 23, 1998, p. 83ff (inset).

9. David Patrick Stearns, "The Sights Are No Match for the Sounds," *USA Today*, March 31, 1998, p. 3D.

10. "People in the News," *U.S. News & World Report*, April 13, 1998, p. 16.

11. James R. Oestreich, "Making a 1712 Cello Sound Less Modern," *New York Times*, February 20, 1999, p. B7.

12. Ibid.

13. Ibid.

14. Helen Wallace, "Out of Place in Baroque World," London *Times*, April 27, 1999.

15. Edith Eisler, "Continuity in Diversity," *Strings*, May/June 2001, p. 50.

CHAPTER 8. LAUNCHING THE SILK ROAD PROJECT

1. Silk Road Project, http://www.silkroadproject.org (February 15, 2003).

2. Beverly Schuch, "Internationally Known Cellist Yo-Yo Ma Continues to Expand His Musical Horizons," *CNN Pinnacle*, August 4, 2001 (transcript).

3. Beth Gardiner, Associated Press, October 16, 1999.

4. Lesley Valdes, "Traveling the Silk Route," *American Record Guide*, November/December 2001, pp. 44ff.

5. Ken Smith, "When Strangers Meet," *Strad*, February 2002, http://www.classicalmusicworld.com/home.asp? magazine=archives (March 3, 2003).

6. Gloria Goodale, "Finding a Musical Route Between East and West," *Christian Science Monitor*, March 9, 2001, p. 18.

7. Smith.

8. Bradley Bambarger, "Classical: Keeping Score," *Billboard*, March 3, 2001.

9. Melinda Bargreen, "Cellist Yo-Yo Ma's Silk Road Project Paves Way for Cross-Cultural Exchanges," *Seattle Times*, May 5, 2002, p. K1.

10. The Silk Road Project website, "Education." Retrieved Dec. 2015, http://archive.silkroadproject.org/Education/EducationOverview/tabid/170/Default.asp.

11. Harvard University website, "The Silk Road Project: Residency at Harvard," posted Nov. 2007, retrieved Dec. 2015, http://www.fas.harvard.edu/~silkroad/index.html.

Chapter 9. More New Adventures

1. T.J. Medrek, "Classical Music: Ma's 'Map' Includes a Return to France," *Boston Herald*, January 17, 2003, p. S09.

2. United Nations, "Secretary-General to Recognize Renowned Cellist Yo-Yo Ma as Messenger of Peace," posted Sept. 2006, retrieved Dec. 2015, http://www.un.org/press/en/2006/note6034.doc.htm.

3. Kim Correro. "Yo-Yo Ma's Recording Songs of Joy & Peace Achieves Best-Ever One-Week Sales of Ma's 30-Year Career with Sony Masterworks," Sony Masterworks, posted Nov. 2008, retrieved Dec. 2015, https://www.sony.com/en_us/SCA/company-news/press-releases/sony-music-masterworks/2008/yo-yo-mas-recording-songs-of-joy-peace-achieves-be.html.

4. The Associated Press, "Quartet at Inauguration Played to Taped Music," posted Jan. 2009, retrieved Dec. 2015, http://www.arkansasonline.com/news/2009/jan/22/quartet-inauguration-played-taped-music/?f=news-politics-elections.

5. NPR Music, "'Self Comes to Mind': Your Brain on Music," posted Dec. 2012, retrieved Dec. 2015, http://www.npr.org/templates/story/story.php?storyId=103713700.

6. President's Committee on the Arts and Humanities, "About Us," retrieved Dec. 2015, http://www.pcah.gov/about-us.

7. Mark Caro, "CSO's Citizen Musician Seeks Right Note," *The Chicago Tribune*, posted March 2013, retrieved Dec. 2015, http://articles.chicagotribune.com/2013-03-04/entertainment/chi-cso-citizen-musician-20130301_1_citizen-musician-cso-riccardo-muti.

8. Mark Caro, "From the Stage to the Streets: Yo-Yo Ma and a Kids Choir Take Over a Train Station, and the Citizen Musician Movement Is Launched," *The Chicago Tribune*, posted Jan. 2011, retrieved Dec. 2015, http://articles.chicagotribune.com/2011-01-30/entertainment/ct-live-0131-cso-around-chicago-20110130_1_yo-yo-ma-association-president-deborah-rutter-cso-music-director.

9. Wendy Fung and Ophelia Wan, "A U.S.-Chinese Cultural Dialogue" Asia Society press release, posted Oct. 2011, retrieved Dec. 2015, http://sites.asiasociety.org/uschinaforum/wp-content/uploads/2011/10/Press-Release-PDF-EN.pdf.

10. Josh Chin, "Big Names in U.S. Culture Take 'Class Trip' to China," *The Wall Street Journal,* China edition, posted Nov. 2011, retrieved Dec. 2015. <http://blogs.wsj.com/chinarealtime/2011/11/15/big-names-in-u-s-culture-take-class-trip-to-china/.

11. The Kennedy Center for the Performing Arts, "The History of the Kennedy Center Honors, retrieved Dec. 2015, <https://www.kennedy-center.org/programs/specialevents/honors/history.cfm.

12. Stacey Federoff, "Cellist Yo-Yo Ma Receives Fred Rogers Award; Event Raises $1M for Center," *Pittsburgh Tribune Review* online, posted May 2014, retrieved Dec. 2015, http://triblive.com/news/westmoreland/6037470-74/rogers-fred-award#axzz3uDfBUhuR.

13. Ibid.

14. Yo-Yo Ma, "Vision Statement," *Silk Road Project*, http://www.silkroadproject.org (September 12, 2003).

15. Stuart Jeffries, "Yo-Yo Ma: Bach, Big Bird, and Me," *The Guardian,* posted July 2015, retrieved Dec. 2015, http://www.theguardian.com/music/2015/jul/28/yo-yo-ma-bach-big-bird-and-me.

16. Justin Davidson, "Have Cello, Will Travel," *Newsday*, November 30, 1997, p. D10.

Glossary

baroque—Of or relating to a dramatic style of music, common in the seventeenth century, that featured many parts and details.

bow—A curved rod with stretched fibers (usually horse-hair) that is drawn across the strings of an instrument to make music.

catalytic—Causing or involving an intense change.

collaborate—To work together.

compatriots—People from the same country, group, or organization.

concerto—A piece of music written to be performed by one or more instruments with an orchestra.

conservatory—A school in which students are taught music, theater, or dance.

contemporary—Beginning or happening in recent times.

humanities—The branch of learning and education that focuses on human qualities and works.

improvise—To speak or perform without preparation or rehearsal.

innovate—To do something in a new way.

movement—A unit of music that is part of a larger composition.

prodigy—A young person who is extremely talented in some way.

quartet—A group of four.

recital—A dance or musical performance.

repertoire—All the pieces that a musician knows how to play or has played.

soloist—One who performs music, or part of an orchestral piece, by him- or herself.

sonata—A piece of music written so that it has sections that are different in rhythm and mood.

submerge—To become fully involved in an activity or interest.

suite—A piece of music made up of many short pieces taken from a larger work.

venues—A place or location where an event occurs.

Further Reading

Books

Buckley, Annie. *Life Skills Biography: Yo-Yo Ma*. North Mankato, MN: Cherry Lake Publishing, 2014.

Ceceri, Kathy. *The Silk Road: Explore the World's Most Famous Trade Route With 20 Projects*. Ann Arbor, MI: Nomad Press, 2011.

Forbes, Andrew. *Insight Guides: The Silk Road*. London: Apa Books, 2012.

Levin, Theodore, et al. (ed.). *The Music of Central Asia*. Bloomington, IN: Indiana University Press, 2016.

Ma, Marina, as told to John A. Rallo. *My Son, Yo-Yo*. New York: Chinese University Press (Columbia University Press), 2012 (Kindle edition).

Websites

Asian American Arts Centre

artspiral.org/about.php

A nonprofit community arts organization for Asian Americans.

The Silk Road Project

silkroadproject.org

Official site of Ma's Silk Road Project.

Yo-Yo Ma Official Site

yo-yoma.com

Everything you need to know about Yo-Yo Ma.

Index